JAPANESE IN MANGALAND

Workbook

1

Marc Bernabé

Manga *Rakujō*

Art: **Gabriel Luque**
Story: **Marc Bernabé**

Translation: Olinda Cordukes

Marc Bernabe (L'Ametlla del Valles, Barcelona, 1976) is a Japanese-Spanish / Catalan translator and interpreter, working mainly on manga and anime translations. Apart from his translation work, he also specializes in language and Japanese culture didactics for foreigners, with a master's degree from the Osaka University of Foreign Studies. His published works are: *Japanese in MangaLand 1, 2* and *3* (Japan Publications Trading Co., Ltd., 2004, 2005 and 2006), the Spanish adaptation of James W. Heisig's *Remembering the kanji* series, and other books on Japan and the Japanese language aimed at the Spanish speaking public. http://www.nipoweb.com

Gabriel Luque (Buenos Aires, Argentina, 1978) is an artist and illustrator, and he contributes to several local media magazines specializing in manga and anime. In 2000 he published his own comic book, *Asesino 55*, and in 2003 he contributed as an illustrator to the books *Japanese in MangaLand*, volumes 2 and 3. He currently spends his time producing storyboards and various illustration projects.

Japanese in MangaLand
Workbook 1
By Marc Bernabe

© 2006 by *Marc Bernabe / Represented by NORMA Editorial S.A.*
Published and distributed: *Japan Publications Trading Co., Ltd.,*
                            1-2-1 Sarugaku-cho, Chiyoda-ku, Tokyo, Japan.

1ˢᵗ printing: July 2006

Overseas Distributors
UNITED STATES:
   Kodansha America, Inc. through Oxford University Press,
   198 Madison Avenue, New York, NY 10016.
CANADA:
   Fitzhenry & Whiteside Ltd., 195 Allstate Parkway, Markham,
   Ontario L3R 4T8.
AUSTRALIA and NEW ZEALAND:
   Bookwise International Pty Ltd.,
   174 Cormack Road, Wingfield, South Australia 5013, Australia.
EUROPE, ASIA and JAPAN:
   Japan Publications Trading Co., Ltd., 1-2-1 Sarugaku-cho,
   Chiyoda-ku, Tokyo, 101-0064 Japan.

ISBN-13: 978-4-88996-208-6
ISBN-10: 4-88996-208-5

Printed in Spain

目次　Index

本書の特徴 Introduction

This book you are holding is, as its title suggests, an exercise book that complements the lessons in the first text of the *Japanese in MangaLand* series. Although the textbook itself has many exercises, it is obvious that in self-teaching any help is welcome. This book, then, offers many more exercises to make the most of the lessons in *Japanese in MangaLand 1*.

You have probably noticed that you must open this book the "Japanese way." That is, the opposite way to how you would open a western style book. This is due to the inclusion of a full-length manga specifically created for it: *Rakujō*. The characteristics of this comic book are identical to any Japanese manga, both in reading direction and in aesthetics. Therefore, we decided to adapt the whole book to the reading direction the Japanese use for their manga; so you will have to turn the pages "the other way around," from right to left.

How to use this book

The book consists of a total of six blocks eight pages each, always preceded by a four page chapter of *Rakujō*. Each block contains the exercises for five lessons from the original textbook: For example, Block 1 includes activities based on lessons 1 to 5; Block 2, lessons 6 to 10; and so on.

There are two ways to use this exercise book: You can either, one, gradually study the textbook –lesson by lesson, along with performing the exercises included– and, after every five lessons, complete the corresponding block in this workbook; or, two, start with this exercise book once you have completed *Japanese in MangaLand 1* in order to lock in all concepts learned, as well as to prepare yourself for *Japanese in MangaLand 2* (the second book in this teaching method). The choice is yours.

Yet, you must bear this in mind: In the textbook we chose to give the student the *rōmaji* transcription of all texts, to make their study easier and to foster, even in lazier students, an interest and motivation to study Japanese. However, if you are holding this exercise book, this means that you are serious about studying, and you are ready to take a step forward. Therefore, here you will not have the support of *rōmaji*. Except for Block 1, where the hiragana and katakana reading are thoroughly practiced, *rōmaji* disappears from the exercise book; so make good use of Block 1, because, if you want to continue with the rest of this workbook, it is essential that you have assimilated and mastered this block first.

To recreate the "atmosphere" you can find in *shōnen* (for boys) and *shōjo* (for girls) manga, we have opted for a "natural" written Japanese, both in the manga and in the exercises. Thus, medium to high difficulty kanji are used, but always with the help of *furigana*. Nevertheless, there is one important exception, that is explained in the following section, "Structure of Each Block," under E, "**Kanji**".

When you finish each block you can correct yourself straight away, as you will find all the answers to the exercises beginning from page 80 and on. Use them as a guide to check whether you have understood the exercises completely. Should you have any doubts, always review the textbook to try to clarify and solve things: Making a mistake and then finding out where your error is, is the best study method.

This exercise book is progressively difficult, which means that in each of the blocks grammatical patterns or vocabulary from previous blocks can appear: Stay alert at all times, slips will not be tolerated!

IMPORTANT: This book is based on the "corrected and expanded edition" of *Japanese in MangaLand 1*, published in 2006. However, if you have the old edition, you don't need to worry: On pages 94 and 95 there is a list with all the explanations and material that does not appear in the book's first editions. Before you start working on each block's exercises, study those materials detailed on pages 94 and 95, so you can embark on the task with the necessary tools.

Structure of each block

Each of the six blocks has twelve pages, in the following order:

A) **RAKUJŌ**. This manga is an original work specifically created for this exercise book. With it, you will be able to really learn Japanese through manga, since the texts have been adapted to what you have learned in each one of the blocks of five lessons from *Japanese in MangaLand 1*. In each chapter, however, some new words appear—these are listed on the fifth page of each block (just after the manga pages). We recommend that you first read and study the new vocabulary; after which, you can then enjoy the manga. You have more information about *Rakujō* on page 7. Should you require it, you can have at your disposal the English translation of all the dialogues ("Japanese in MangaLand" – "Workbook 1"), which can be found at www.nipoweb.com.

B) **READING COMPREHENSION**. On these two pages you will be asked questions on the *Rakujō* chapter you have just read. By means of these exercises you will be able to check to what extent you have understood the text and the development of the story.

c) **VOCABULARY**. Two pages with several kinds of exercises with which to practice the vocabulary you have learned in each block (and to review that of previous blocks).

D) **GRAMMAR**. Two pages with several kinds of exercises with which to reinforce those grammatical patterns learned in each block (and to review those of previous blocks).

E) **KANJI**. Two pages with which to practice reading, writing, and the use of kanji in its

context. Be very careful, because this part is not based on the lessons, but on the textbook's "Compilation of Kanji." Still, we have always tried to select those kanji which are related in some way to each block's contents. Each "Kanji" section is headed by a list of twenty-two characters, except for Block 1 (which has only eighteen). Underneath each kanji there is a number that corresponds to its entry in the "Compilation of Kanji" in *Japanese in MangaLand 1*. Before doing the exercises, you should thoroughly study those twenty-two kanji in the aforementioned compilation; otherwise, making the most of this section will be difficult.

Attention: We had better warn you that, since this book becomes progressively difficult, once a kanji has been thoroughly studied in a block, it will <u>always</u> appear without *furigana* in subsequent blocks. Thus, you will have to make an effort to read it by heart every time it appears (which will obviously be very positive for your study).

Acknowledgements

Years go by, and the *Japanese in MangaLand* project keeps developing more and more with new material; even on an international scope, as the series has been translated into various languages. And those to thank are, mainly, you... the readers. You are the ones who made me realize a book with additional exercises could be an ideal supplement for the textbook, and you encouraged me to work on it. Now that it is in your hands, I hope you won't be disappointed, and that you can make the most of it. As far as I'm concerned, I have put all my eggs in one basket, to obtain the best possible result.

I have much to thank **Gabriel Luque**, an excellent artist who has contributed with all his passion to the creation of the manga *Rakujō*, and to **Veronica Calafell**, who has had an important, if not essential, role in the making of this project: thanks to her wide experience in the field of teaching, she has helped me to come up with the exercises which fill these pages, so that they were varied, enjoyable, and, above all, useful. I also want to thank my pleasant professor 小林明美 **Akemi Kobayashi**, who supported me during the making of this book, as well as 徳永恵美香 **Emika Tokunaga** and **Alberto Aldarabí**, who went through the book, so it would be perfect before its printing. Translator **Olinda Cordukes** and proofreader and friend **Daniel Carmona** made possible this English version; many thanks to them too. As usual, **Japan Publications Trading** and **Norma Editorial** must not be excluded from these acknowledgements: Without them, this book would not be on the shelves of bookstores today. Finally, a very special wink to the **Saizeriya** restaurant in Ishibashi, where all the exercises in this book were brewed at countless "brainstorm dinners."

Marc Bernabé

Osaka, 24th of July, 2005

落城 Rakujō

The story takes place on the distant planet of Saka, which was devastated by the defeat in a war a few years earlier. Nevertheless, Saka still has an air of splendor, which is a remnant of its once highly developed civilization and which is an echo of its once regal reign over the galaxy. The Saka base is an apparently impregnable and great fortress where its leaders Yodo and her son, Hide, are taking refuge. The governor of the galaxy, Yasu, is looking for an excuse to attack and to end, once and for all, the threats to resist the clutches of his tyrannical grip. However, in opposition to his plans for purging the planet of rebelliousness, he finds fierce general Yuki, who arrives with his troops to defend the last fortress...

Characters

YUKI: Brave and faithful general, loyal to the clan headed by Hide and Yodo.

YODO: A woman of strong character, she excels in beauty as equally as she does in obstinacy. She is mother to Hide, and is relentless in imposing her own opinions upon him.

HIDE: Young leader of the planet Saka. Being a rather timid and fainthearted man, he tends to let himself be persuaded by his mother's overbearing will.

YASU: Present governor of the galaxy, an extremely cunning and ruthless strategist. He is not prepared to let anybody prevent him from gaining absolute control over the galaxy.

Yuki   Yodo   Hide   Yasu

How to read the manga

Manga is read "the other way around" compared to how a Western comic book is read; that is, from right to left, including balloons and panels. If you are used to reading manga published in Eastern reading order, you won't have trouble reading *Rakujō*. Otherwise, it may take a couple of tries before you get used to this way of reading.

Watch out: When the sides of the panel are painted **black**, what is narrated in these panels takes place in a different temporal period to that of the story being told; that is, these panels take place either in the past or in the future.

これはセキュリティーエリアのマップです

山

北
きた

東
ひがし

西
にし

南
みなみ

ヤス第一アーミー
だいいち
八万九千三百五十四人
にん

サカ基地
きち

セキュリティーエリア

ヤス第三アーミー
だいさん
15万321人
にん

ヤス第二アーミー
だいに
123628人
にん

山
やま

川
かわ

山
やま

Block 1: Lessons 1-5

Important: We are assuming that you have already mastered both of the Japanese syllabaries, hiragana and katakana, to perfection. Therefore, you won't have the help of *rōmaji* throughout this exercise book. If you still feel uncomfortable with the syllabaries, we recommend that you study them thoroughly first, and then do the hiragana and katakana practice exercises on pages 14 to 17. Once you have mastered them, start doing the exercises of this block's first two pages.

RAKUJŌ — New vocabulary 新しい単語

しょう 章	chapter	area エリア	area
きち 基地	(military) base	map マップ	map
leader リーダー	leader	army アーミー	army
security セキュリティー	security		

1. Based on what you have read in the first chapter of *Rakujō*, what action do you think the following onomatopoeia represent?

カッカッカッカッ	_____	わはははは	_____
ゴゴゴゴゴ	_____	ドカ ー ン	_____
ガキィィィン	_____	ひゅ ——	_____

2. What is the name of the man who introduces himself to Hide at the end of page 3?

3. How many men make up Yasu's first army? How about the third army?

4. Read in Japanese the figures indicating the number of men in Yasu's armies.

5. Choose the right answer.

a) What greeting would you use at 2 PM?

　　1.こんばんは　②こんにちは　3.こんにちわ　4.こんぱんは

b) What do you say when you go to bed at night?

　　1.おやすみなさい　2.おはよう　3.こんばんは　4.バイバイ

c) If you had to congratulate someone, what expression would you use?

　　1.すみません　2.じゃね、また　3.おめでとうございます　4.どうも

d) How would a young man say goodbye to a class mate whom he'll be seeing soon?

　　1.またね！　2.さようなら！　3.まだね！　4.ごめんなさい！

e) What is the standard answer to the greeting お元気ですか？

　　1.まあ、ね　2.はい、元気です　3.気をつけて　4.よろしくお願いします

6. A friend says ありがとう！to you. What do you answer? And what do you answer if a person you hardly know says ありがとうございます？

7. What is the meaning of 気をつけて, and in what kind of situations do we use it?

8. It's 8 AM, and you go into a store. Reproduce the conversation you have with the storekeeper, following the guide we give you.

You:	おはようございます	(Good morning)
Storekeeper:	_____	(Welcome)
You:	_____	(How much is this?)
Storekeeper:	_____	(This is 343 yen)
You:	_____	(383 yen?)
Storekeeper:	_____	(No, 343 yen)
You:	_____	(I'll take this, please)
Storekeeper:	_____	(Thank you very much)
You:	_____	(You are welcome)
Storekeeper:	_____	(Goodbye)
You:	_____	(Goodbye)

9. Develop the stroke order of the following characters, as in the example.

た	ニ	ナ	た	た	ふ				
あ	ニ	ナ			き				
む	ニ				え				
ゆ					ち				
す					ね				
は					を				
お					ま				
け					か				

10. Link each hiragana character with its corresponding reading in *rōmaji*.

の → no	mi	ちゃ	zu	
き	sa	ぺ	cha	
く	ku	じょ	ne	
さ	no	づ	wa	
じ	pa	わ	ga	
し	ji	が	zu	
み	ki	ず	jo	
ぱ	shi	ね	pe	

11. Transcribe each hiragana character into *rōmaji* and vice versa.

い __i__	う ___	じゅ ___	to __と__	be ___	chu ___
ぞ ___	な ___	ちゃ ___	o ___	go ___	rya ___
ぽ ___	ぬ ___	りょ ___	pe ___	wa ___	gyu ___
か ___	を ___	きゃ ___	ru ___	zu ___	ja ___
り ___	ん ___	みゅ ___	mo ___	shi ___	byo ___

12. Transcribe the following words in hiragana into *rōmaji*.

おんがく	<u>ongaku</u>	いちご	_____	つなみ	_____
さかな	_____	ちゃのゆ	_____	でんしゃ	_____
りょかん	_____	いしばし	_____	くいだおれ	_____
いいわけ	_____	けいさつかん	_____	ふつかよい	_____
したぎ	_____	いきじごく	_____	かみのけ	_____
どろぼう	_____	とうきょう	_____	きっぱり	_____
くうしゅう	_____	ぎょうざ	_____	まっちゃ	_____
がんりゅう	_____	さっぽろ	_____	きょうみ	_____
したっぱ	_____	ぎゅうにゅう	_____	いろっぽい	_____

13. Transcribe the following words in *rōmaji* into hiragana.

nihongo	<u>にほんご</u>	meitantei	_____	jitabata	_____
shamisen	_____	nemawashi	_____	kannushi	_____
nagoyaka	_____	tsuyu	_____	tabako	_____
tanpopo	_____	pakuri	_____	ebisu	_____
momiage	_____	tebukuro	_____	donzoko	_____
kyūri	_____	jakkan	_____	assari	_____
jūdō	_____	kenkyū	_____	buchō	_____
gunyagunya	_____	kyūshū	_____	yappari	_____
kyakka	_____	nyōi	_____	kyūdō	_____

14. If there are any mistakes in the following transcriptions, correct them.

かがや	ka~~k~~ ^gaya	おのはら	anohara	あっぱれ	appawa
こっぱ	kobba	さぼてん	kiboten	はだか	hodaka
ぶらり	purari	こわっぱ	koneppa	うねりごえ	unerigoe
りょうつう	ryōtsū	のうぎょう	nūgyō	まみれ	momiwa

–15– ひらがな Hiragana

15. Develop the stroke order of the following characters, as in the example.

ホ	一 ﾉ 一	十 二	オ	ホ	シ				
チ					ク				
サ					ウ				
ロ					メ				
マ					ソ				
ヨ					ン				
ナ					ラ				
ネ					オ				

16. Link each katakana character with its corresponding reading in *rōmaji*.

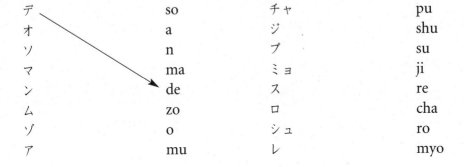

デ	so	チャ	pu
オ	a	ジ	shu
ソ	n	プ	su
マ	ma	ミョ	ji
ン	de	ス	re
ム	zo	ロ	cha
ゾ	o	シュ	ro
ア	mu	レ	myo

17. Transcribe each katakana character into *rōmaji* and vice versa.

カ __ka__	エ ___	ギュ ___	ze ___ゼ	no ___	pyu ___
ド ___	ワ ___	リャ ___	u ___	n ___	ja ___
ツ ___	フ ___	チャ ___	ke ___	wa ___	myo ___
メ ___	ク ___	ピョ ___	ji ___	yu ___	byu ___
ル ___	ポ ___	ジョ ___	bi ___	mi ___	sho ___

18. Transcribe the following words in katakana into *rōmaji*.

パンダ	_panda_	ミルク	_____	ワシントン	_____
ロリコン	_____	ピアノ	_____	ゼネラル	_____
ギャル	_____	ジャンボ	_____	タンゴ	_____
マラソン	_____	ギリシア	_____	ソンシツ	_____
オランダ	_____	シャワー	_____	ギブアップ	_____
キャラバン	_____	クリーナー	_____	ハーモニー	_____
バグダッド	_____	ルノアール	_____	フットボール	_____
キューピッド	_____	マトリックス	_____	チャーミング	_____
マスコット	_____	アットマーク	_____	ホットポット	_____

19. Transcribe the following words in *rōmaji* into katakana.

furansu	_フランス_	shatsu	_____	gurume	_____
pasokon	_____	arabama	_____	igirisu	_____
maiwaifu	_____	neruson	_____	myunhen	_____
remon	_____	kyaria	_____	napori	_____
nūdo	_____	apaato	_____	gyappu	_____
kōhii	_____	kūdetaa	_____	raamen	_____
pureeyaa	_____	kukkii	_____	piramiddo	_____
chachacha	_____	biitoruzu	_____	kyasshu	_____
supittsu	_____	jaanarisuto	_____	doraiyaa	_____

20. If there are any mistakes in the following transcriptions, correct them.

シューマイ	sh<u>ū</u>mai	ソナタ	tsunata	レバー	rebaa
ミスター	misukū	アンドラ	asodora	メキシコ	mekinko
ノウハウ	souhawa	ケース	keenu	キャンセル	kyanseru
ビッグマン	pigguman	サッカー	sakkaa	ナニワ	naniu

一	二	三	四	五	六	七	八	九
(1)	(2)	(3)	(4)	(5)	(6)	(7)	(8)	(9)
十	百	千	万	円	東	西	南	北
(10)	(11)	(12)	(13)	(14)	(29)	(30)	(31)	(32)

21. Develop the stroke order of the following kanji.

南	一	十	一十					
四	丨							
円								
北								
万								

22. Link each kanji with its meaning.

東 ——————→ East
六　　　　　　South
万　　　　　　six
円　　　　　　ten thousand
南　　　　　　yen
一　　　　　　one

百　　　　　　West
九　　　　　　ten
西　　　　　　nine
北　　　　　　hundred
二　　　　　　North
十　　　　　　two

23. Link each kanji with its most common reading.

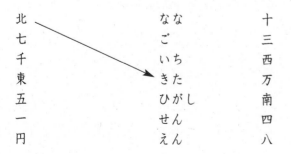

北　　　　　なな
七　　　　　ご
千　　　　　いち
東　　　　　きた
五　　　　　ひがし
一　　　　　せん
円　　　　　えん

十　　　　　みなみ
三　　　　　さん
西　　　　　よん
万　　　　　はち
南　　　　　まん
四　　　　　じゅう
八　　　　　にし

24. Write the following numbers in kanji and give their reading in *furigana*.

8	八 (はち)	3	_____	9	_____
16	_____	12	_____	24	_____
35	_____	47	_____	50	_____
88	_____	111	_____	897	_____
7,200	_____	3,874	_____	1,011 ·	_____

25. Give the reading of the following numbers, and write their figures in Arabic numerals.

三	さん (3)	五	_____ ( )
十九	_____ ( )	八十	_____ ( )
五十八	_____ ( )	九十五	_____ ( )
百二	_____ ( )	三百五十七	_____ ( )
八千五十一	_____ ( )	千二百三十三	_____ ( )

26. Write the following numbers in kanji and give their reading in *furigana*.

3,783	三千七百八十三 (さんぜんななひゃくはちじゅうさん)	10,940	_____
24,851	_____	300,340	_____
834,901	_____	108,234	_____
560,205	_____	1,280,785	_____
75,034,026	_____	834,201,016	_____

27. Give the reading of the following numbers, and write their figures in Arabic numerals.

二万六千二百三	にまんろくせんにひゃくさん	(26,203)
五万七百二十九	_____	( )
十八万五千五百三十二	_____	( )
三百八十七万五千二百十四	_____	( )
二億三千二百万五千百十二	_____	( )

しかし、十日に
台風が来ます。

雨が降りはじめました。

十日か…

それはサカ基地の
キャノンです。

ライフルではありませんでした。
キャノンでした。

きみ、これは何?

キャノン?ライフル
じゃなかった?

ザ

RAKUJŌ — New vocabulary 新しい単語

銀河 (ぎんが)	galaxy	キャノン (cannon)	cannon
サイボーグ (cyborg)	cyborg	ライフル (rifle)	rifle
ロボット (robot)	robot	キャンプ (camp)	camp
メガ (mega)	mega- (prefix)	よし！	All right!
ファイト (fight)	fight	アタック (attack)	attack
ヴァイオレント (violent)	violent	わかりました	Sure, I get you
外 (そと)	outside	敵 (てき)	enemy
しかし	however	サー (sir)	sir
来ます	to come	バンザイ (万歳)	hurrah!

1. Based on what you have read in the second chapter of *Rakujō*, in what year of the Western calendar does the action take place?

2. What's the present weather like at the Saka base? (Say it in Japanese.)

3. What will happen in four days, weather-wise?

4. Which personal pronoun does Hide use when he talks to Yuki? How about Yodo when she talks to Yuki? Why do you think they use these specific pronouns and not a different one?

5. Does Hide conjugate the verb です in the simple form or in the formal form when he speaks with Yuki? Why do you think he speaks this way?

6. In what form is Hide's sentence ライフルじゃなかった conjugated? Specify all possible conjugations for this sentence:

Simple present	_____
Formal present	_____ライフルです_____
Simple past	_____
Formal past	_____
Simple negative	_____
Simple negative (2)	_____
Formal negative	_____
Simple past negative	_____
Simple past negative (2)	_____
Formal past negative	_____
Formal past negative (2)	_____

7. Write down Yuki's answer to Hide's question ライフルじゃなかった？. Change this answer into the interrogative in both forms, simple and formal.

8. Based on L.8 and using as an example some of the English origin based words in katakana that we have seen in this chapter of *Rakujō*, try transcribing the following words into katakana.

cybot	___ザイボット___	shake	_____
cybernet	_____	fake	_____
scandal	_____	venus	_____
ham	_____	guerrilla	_____
check	_____	tiramisu	_____

9. Translate the following dates into Japanese. Don't forget to specify as well their reading in *furigana*, as in the example.

13th of March   さんがつじゅうさんにち ３月１３日   4th of April   _____

12th of June   _____   10th of August   _____

6th of May   _____   26th of January   _____

17th of July   _____   1st of December   _____

20th of September   _____   24th of February   _____

10. Knowing well the "Japanese eras" (based on the reign of the emperors) is important to be able to correctly interpret those dates written in the classical way, which are still commonly referred to even nowadays. According to what you studied in L.6, to what years of the Western calendar do the following Japanese years correspond?

へいせい　ねん
平成１７年   _____2005_____   しょうわ　ねん
昭和３０年   _____

めいじ　ねん
明治５年   _____   へいせい　ねん
平成２年   _____

たいしょう　ねん
大正１０年   _____   しょうわ　ねん
昭和５１年   _____

11. Link the following words based on their similarity in concept or association of ideas. In this exercise, we have used a Japanese perspective; therefore, you must bear in mind the passage of seasons in Japan (check L.10 if you have any doubts).

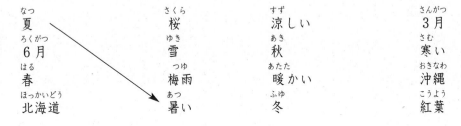

なつ
夏   さくら
桜   すず
涼しい   さんがつ
３月

ろくがつ
６月   ゆき
雪   あき
秋   さむ
寒い

はる
春   つゆ
梅雨   あたた
暖かい   おきなわ
沖縄

ほっかいどう
北海道   あつ
暑い   ふゆ
冬   こうよう
紅葉

12. Place the pronouns in the table on the right in their corresponding box.

	singular	plural
1st person	わたし 私	
2nd person		

わたし
私̶   あなた

まえ
お前ら   ぼく
僕

きみ
君   おれ
俺たち

われわれ   わし

まえ
お前   あんたたち

てんきよほう
天気予報
Weather forecast

13. Complete these simple sentences with the missing word. You can write Japanese place names in hiragana or, if you know them, in kanji.

おおさか は
大阪は___晴れ___です

あらし
_____は嵐です

おきなわ
沖縄は_____ではありません

きゅうしゅう
九州は_____です

くも
_____は曇りです (1)

くも
_____は曇りです (2 op.)

ほっかいどう
北海道は_____です

ひろしま
広島は_____ではありません

14. Transcribe these words into katakana according to the rules studied in lessons 2 and 8.

Randy   ___ランディー___   Sylvia   _____

California   _____   George   _____

Chuck   _____   Dionysus   _____

Constantinople   _____   Stephanie   _____

Canyon   _____   Jodie   _____

第二部

15. Choose the right answer.

a) ＿＿＿はボールペンです。

    1.その　2.それ　3.あそこ　4.あの

b) ＿＿＿に筆がある。（ある＝"there is/are"）

    1.あそこ　2.あれ　3.この　4.これ

c) 彼女^{かのじょ}は＿＿＿ですか。

    1.この　2.どの　3.あれ　4.どこ

d) ＿＿＿は何^{なん}ですか。

    1.あれ　2.どの　3.この　4.どれ

16. Complete the following sentences with the most suitable *kosoado* pronoun.

a) ＿＿＿は写真^{しゃしん}です。 (close to the speaker)

b) ＿＿＿は雪^{ゆき}ですか。 (far from both interlocutors)

c) ＿＿＿に鳥^{とり}がいる。 ("there is/are;" close to the speaker)

d) A: ボールペンはどこですか。 | B: ＿＿＿だ！ (close to the listener)

e) A: ＿＿＿人^{ひと}が先生^{せんせい}ですか。 | B: あの人^{ひと}です。 (far from both interlocutors)

f) ＿＿＿犬^{いぬ}はばかです！(close to the speaker)

17. Follow the instructions and conjugate the correct form of the verb です in each case.

a) あれはテーブル＿＿でした＿＿。 (formal past)

b) その人^{ひと}は学生^{がくせい}＿＿＿＿。 /＿＿＿＿。 (formal negative; 2 options)

c) 今日^{きょう}は土曜日^{どようび}＿＿＿＿。 (formal interrogative)

d) これはお金^{かね}＿＿＿＿。 /＿＿＿＿。 (simple negative; 2 options)

e) その人^{ひと}は先生^{せんせい}＿＿＿＿。 /＿＿＿＿。 (formal neg. interrog.; 2 opt.)

f) それは一万円＿＿＿＿。 (simple past)

g) その猫^{ねこ}はばか＿＿＿＿。 /＿＿＿＿。 (simple past neg.; 2 options)

h) あれはレモン＿＿＿＿。 (formal past interrogative)

旅行予定

| 3日(日) 東京（とうきょう） |
| 4日(月) ロンドン |
| 5日(火) ローマ |
| 6日(水) バルセロナ |
| 7日(木) パリ |
| 8日(金) アムステルダム |
| 9日(土) 上海（シャンハイ） |

18. Mr. Akiyama has to go on a business trip around several cities in the world. Bearing in mind his travel plans (specified on the piece of paper on the left), complete the following sentences. Fill in the blanks with the correct kanji and add the reading of the kanji you write.

a) 秋山（あきやま）さんは火曜日（かようび）に＿ローマ＿です。

b) むいか（ 六日 ）は ＿水曜日（すいようび）＿ です。(day)

c) 秋山（あきやま）さんは＿＿＿＿＿にパリです。(2 opt.)

d) ＿＿＿＿＿は土曜日（どようび）です。

e) 秋山（あきやま）さんは日曜日（にちようび）に＿＿＿＿＿です。

f) 秋山（あきやま）さんはいつか（ 　　 ）に＿＿＿＿＿です。

g) 秋山（あきやま）さんはよっか（ 　　 ）にアムステルダム＿＿＿＿＿＿。

h) 秋山（あきやま）さんはここのか（ 　　 ）に＿＿＿＿＿です。

i) ようか（ 　　 ）は＿＿＿＿＿じゃありません。

19. Complete with the appropriate personal pronoun in each case, choosing it from the box below.

a) ＿私（わたし）＿の名前（なまえ）はトモコです。(1st sing. | woman, to a stranger)

b) ＿＿＿＿の名前（なまえ）は山田（やまだ）と秋本（あきもと）です。(1st pl. | politicians, among them)

c) ＿＿＿＿の名前（なまえ）は風之介（かぜのすけ）です。(1st sing. | samurai, to a stranger)

d) ＿＿＿＿の名前（なまえ）は何（なん）ですか。(2nd sing. | 40-year-old man, to a young woman)

e) ＿＿＿＿の名前（なまえ）はエミカです。(3rd sing. | girl, to a stranger)

f) ＿＿＿＿はばかじゃない！(1st pl. | young men, to some friends)

g) ＿＿＿＿はばかだった (3rd pl. | young men, among them)

| 彼ら（かれら） | 君（きみ） | 私（わたし）〔取り消し〕 | 俺ら（おれら） | 彼女（かのじょ） | 拙者（せっしゃ） | われわれ |

-29- 文法 Grammar

日	月	火	水	木	金	土	春	夏	秋	冬
(16)	(17)	(18)	(19)	(20)	(21)	(22)	(86)	(87)	(88)	(89)
年	人	男	女	子	私	山	川	田	本	雨
(54)	(15)	(33)	(34)	(35)	(82)	(42)	(43)	(44)	(74)	(138)

20. Develop the stroke order of the following kanji.

水					
男					
年					
春					
雨					

21. Link each kanji with its most common reading (usually, the *kun'yomi*).

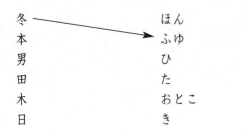

冬	ほん	人	ひと
本	ふゆ	秋	あき
男	ひ	夏	かわ
田	た	火	こ
木	おとこ	子	ひ
日	き	川	なつ

22. Indicate the correct kanji or kanji combination for each reading.

a) はる

  1.春　2.巻　3.春　4.泰

b) つき

  1.日　2.目　3.月　4.円

c) だんじょ

  1.男子　2.男女　3.男山　4.男人

d) わたし

  1.利　2.秋　3.科　4.私

23. Indicate the correct reading for each kanji combination.

a) 木曜日

   1.どようび　2.げつようび　3.きんようび　4.もくようび

b) 日本人

   1.にっぽんしん　2.にっぽんじん　3.にほんしん　4.にはんじん

c) 雨水

   1.あめみず　2.あまみす　3.あまみず　4.あめみづ

24. Provide in hiragana the readings of the following words, and give their meaning.

人	ひと	person	秋	_____	_____
山	_____	_____	平成 3 年 (へいせい)	_____	_____
女子	_____	_____	水曜日 (よう)	_____	_____
春休み (やす)	_____	_____	六日	_____	_____
冬眠 (みん)	_____	_____	油田 (ゆ)	_____	_____

25. Write the following words in kanji, and give their meaning.

なつ	夏	summer	おんな	_____	_____
つき	_____	_____	かわ	_____	_____
あめ	_____	_____	か曜び (よう)	_____	_____
しがつ	_____	_____	わたし	_____	_____
はつか	_____	_____	ごねん	_____	_____

26. Correct either the reading or writing mistakes in the following words.

日曜日 (よう)	にちよう~~び~~	日木	にほん	年金	としかね
上曜日 (よう)	どようび	冬休み (やす)	なつやすみ	全曜日 (よう)	きんよび
月曜日	にちようび	火出	かざん	女了	じょし

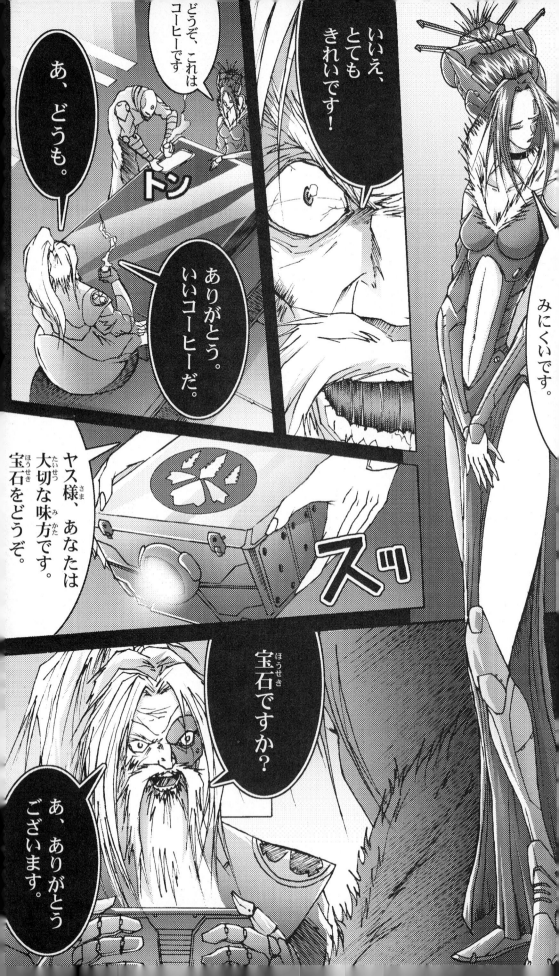

Block 3: Lessons 11-15

RAKUJŌ — New vocabulary 新しい単語

会議 (かいぎ)	meeting	宝石 (ほうせき)	precious stone, jewel
忙しい (いそが)	busy (-*i* adj.)	個 (こ)	counter for small things
最近 (さいきん)	lately	無理な (む り)	impossible (-*na* adj.)
昔 (むかし)	long ago	頼み (たの)	request
みにくい	ugly (-*i* adj.)	戦争 (せんそう)	war
とても	very	来る (く)	to come
味方 (みかた)	ally	強い (つよ)	strong (-*i* adj.)

1. Based on what you have read in the third chapter of *Rakujō*, what proper name suffix does Yasu use when he talks to Yodo? Why do you think he uses this one?

2. What proper name suffix does Yodo use towards Yasu? Why do you think she has chosen this one? What are its connotations? How about Yasu, when he talks about Hide, what suffix does he add after his name? Why?

3. At what time does the meeting between Yodo and Yasu which opens the chapter take place? Give the reading of this time and indicate an alternative way of saying it. In addition, at what time does Yasu say he will return the next day? Give the reading and indicate, as well, an alternative way of saying it.

4. Make a list of all the *-i* and *-na* adjectives that appear in this third chapter of *Rakujō*.

-i adjectives	*-na* adjectives
_____	_____
_____	_____
_____	_____
_____	_____
_____	_____

5. Conjugate these two adjectives into the different forms indicated.

みにくいです	formal present affirmative	きれいです
_____	simple present affirmative	_____
_____	formal past affirmative	_____
_____	simple past affirmative	_____
_____	formal present negative	_____
_____	simple present negative	_____
_____	formal past negative	_____
_____	simple past negative	_____

6. Yodo, in one of her sentences, says 大切な味方. Shortly after, Yasu adds 大切じゃなかった. Why does the first sentence keep the な of the *-na* adjective, and the second sentence doesn't?

7. What is the misunderstanding between Yodo and Yasu about, which makes Yasu very furious, so much so that he decides to declare war?

8. What are counters and what do we use them for? Analyzing the context of the third chapter, what do you think 個 means?

9. Pick only the mammals from this list and mark them with a circle.

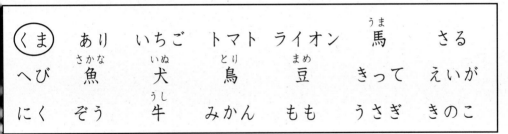

10. Link each store with the article it sells.

八百屋	もも	魚屋	魚
本屋	やさい	果物屋	カメラ
肉屋	ざっし	電気屋	レタス
文房具屋	かみ	八百屋	ごはん
果物屋	にく	レストラン	みかん

11. Complete the sentences with the words in the box below.

a) バナナは＿＿＿＿＿＿＿＿です。

b) ＿＿＿＿＿＿＿＿は赤いです。

c) あの犬は黒くないです。＿＿＿＿＿＿＿＿です。

d) ＿＿＿＿＿＿＿＿は黄色いです。

e) 空は黄色くないです。＿＿＿＿＿＿＿＿です。

f) ＿＿＿＿＿＿＿＿トマトが大好きです。

黄色い	青い	レモン	いちご	赤い	白い

12. Change the words whose meaning does not fit in the following sentences with other words that fit in with the context.

a) ももは ~~やさい~~ くだもの です。   b) なしは果物ではありません。

c) りんごは黒いです。   d) ぞうは大きくないです。

e) 日本の夏は暑くないです。   f) レモンは白いです。

13. Tell what time it is on each clock. Write the time in kanji, indicating (when possible) the two alternative ways of saying the same time, and adding their reading in *furigana*. Finally, translate the sentence into English.

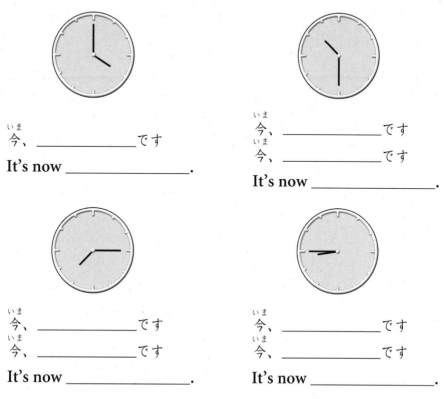

<ruby>今<rt>いま</rt></ruby>、＿＿＿＿＿＿＿です

It's now ＿＿＿＿＿＿＿＿.

<ruby>今<rt>いま</rt></ruby>、＿＿＿＿＿＿＿です
<ruby>今<rt>いま</rt></ruby>、＿＿＿＿＿＿＿です

It's now ＿＿＿＿＿＿＿＿.

<ruby>今<rt>いま</rt></ruby>、＿＿＿＿＿＿＿です
<ruby>今<rt>いま</rt></ruby>、＿＿＿＿＿＿＿です

It's now ＿＿＿＿＿＿＿＿.

<ruby>今<rt>いま</rt></ruby>、＿＿＿＿＿＿＿です
<ruby>今<rt>いま</rt></ruby>、＿＿＿＿＿＿＿です

It's now ＿＿＿＿＿＿＿＿.

14. Complete the following sentences according to the example.

a) **14:00 h** │ <ruby>今<rt>いま</rt></ruby>、＿<ruby>午後<rt>ごご</rt></ruby>＿の＿<ruby>二時<rt>にじ</rt></ruby>＿です。

b) **07:30 h** │ <ruby>今<rt>いま</rt></ruby>、＿＿＿＿＿の＿＿＿＿＿＿です。

c) **02:15 h** │ <ruby>今<rt>いま</rt></ruby>、＿＿＿＿＿の＿＿＿＿＿＿です。

d) **19:45 h** │ <ruby>今<rt>いま</rt></ruby>、＿＿＿＿＿の＿＿＿＿＿＿です。

e) **05:58 h** │ <ruby>今<rt>いま</rt></ruby>、＿＿＿＿＿の＿＿＿＿＿＿です。

f) **22:24 h** │ <ruby>今<rt>いま</rt></ruby>、＿＿＿＿＿の＿＿＿＿＿＿です。

15. What four different meanings can the following sentence have? Why?

a) これはぶたです。

1) ＿＿＿＿＿＿ 2) ＿＿＿＿＿＿ 3) ＿＿＿＿＿＿ 4) ＿＿＿＿＿＿

16. Indicate the correct answer.

a) あの家は＿＿＿＿＿くないです。
 1.小さく　2.小さな　3.小さ　4.小さい

b) 私はやさいが好き＿＿＿＿＿なかった。
 1.じゃ　2.く　3.ではな　4.でわ

c) 小林くんは＿＿＿＿＿です。
 1.親切な　2.親切だ　3.親切　4.親切い

d) ＿＿＿＿＿お茶がきらいでした。
 1.暖かいな　2.暖かいかった　3.暖かくなかい　4.暖かい

17. Conjugate the adjectives into the correct form in each case.

a) この自転車は(赤い)＿赤かったです＿。 (formal past affirmative)

b) あのカメラは(高い)＿＿＿＿＿＿＿。 (simple past negative)

c) キミコちゃんは(きれいな)＿＿＿＿＿＿＿。 (formal present affirmative)

d) その山は(低い)＿＿＿＿＿＿＿。 (formal present negative)

e) あのラーメン屋は(大きい)＿＿＿＿＿＿＿。 (simple present affirmative)

f) 私は(静かな)＿＿＿＿＿庭が(好きな)＿＿＿＿＿。 (simple present affirmative)

g) 古い映画が(きらいな)＿＿＿＿＿＿＿。 (formal past negative)

18. Rewrite each sentence so that it ends having the same meaning.

a) この家は新しいです。
　　この家は ＿古くないです＿。

b) この試験はむずかしいです。
　　この試験は＿＿＿＿＿＿＿。

c) その馬は大きくなかった。
　　その馬は＿＿＿＿＿＿＿。

d) あのたてものは危険でした。
　　あのたてものは＿＿＿＿＿＿＿。

e) 神戸の肉は高かったです。
　　神戸の肉は＿＿＿＿＿＿＿。

f) 彼は魚が好きではない。
　　彼は魚が＿＿＿＿＿＿＿。

g) 富士山は高い山です。
　　富士山は＿＿＿＿＿＿＿。

h) 大阪のラーメン屋は上手じゃない。
　　大阪のラーメン屋は＿＿＿＿＿＿＿。

19. Arrange the following portions to form a correct sentence.

a) 安い | ボールペン | これは | です。 _____これは安いボールペンです_____

b) 上手(な) | 川田さんは | でした。 _____

c) 川本さんは | 人 | でした | きれい(な)。 _____

d) あの | 高かった | りんごは | です。 _____

e) 女は | その | ではありません | きれい(な)。 _____

f) 山田さんの家は | 暗くない | です | 家。 _____

20. Correct any mistakes there might be in the following sentences.

a) あの車は安いではないでした。

b) あれは有名おかしやだ。

c) 私は暗いな教室がきらいでわありません。

d) 山田さんの家は暗い家ではない。

e) その安全じゃないなレストランは大きいじゃないかった。

21. Complete the following sentences with the proper name suffixes you find in the box below.

a) こんにちは、アキオ _さん_ 。(talking to someone we don't know very well)

b) マリ_____、元気？ (adult to a little girl)

c) 坂本_____、忙しいですか？ (student to his or her teacher)

d) アキラ_____、これは何？ (young girl to a friend)

e) 新之助_____は有名ですか？ (samurai to another samurai)

f) 前田_____、お元気ですか？ (storekeeper to a client)

g) 大丈夫ですか、北山_____？ (company employee to his or her director)

くん	先生	殿	社長	~~くん~~	ちゃん	様

今	分	時	半	朝	昼	夜	午	前	後	好
(57)	(53)	(59)	(90)	(46)	(47)	(48)	(58)	(55)	(56)	(146)
白	赤	青	大	小	高	安	新	古	明	方
(71)	(72)	(73)	(49)	(50)	(83)	(84)	(104)	(105)	(159)	(65)

22. Develop the stroke order of the following kanji.

高						
前						
赤						
時						
後						

23. Link each kanji with its most common reading (usually, the *kun'yomi*).

昼	ふるい	高い	ちいさい
古い	やすい	大きい	たかい
青い	あさ	時	じ
朝	ひる	小さい	おおきい
夜	あおい	赤い	あかい
安い	よる	半	はん

24. Indicate the correct kanji or kanji combination for each reading.

a) あかるい

　1.朋るい　2.明るい　3.朋い　4.明い

b) ことし

　1.今年　2.令年　3.分年　4.公年

c) しろい

　1.自い　2.日い　3.目い　4.白い

d) あたらしい

　1.親しい　2.新しい　3.親い　4.新い

25. Indicate the correct reading for each kanji combination.

a) 古本

    1.ふるぽん 2.ふるほん 3.こぽん 4.こほん

b) 好きな

    1.あきな 2.こきな 3.きらきな 4.すきな

c) 午前

    1.ごまえ 2.ごご 3.ごぜん 4.ごあと

26. Provide in hiragana the readings of the following words, and give their meaning.

古い	<u>ふるい</u>	<u>old</u>	五分	_____	_____
六分	_____	_____	三時半	_____	_____
高い	_____	_____	人前	_____	_____
前半	_____	_____	半分	_____	_____
青春	_____	_____	文明	_____	_____

27. Write the following words in kanji, and give their meaning.

あおい	青い	<u>blue</u>	やすい	_____	_____
あさ	_____	_____	かた	_____	_____
おおきい	_____	_____	いま	_____	_____
あかい	_____	_____	ごご	_____	_____
せいねん	_____	_____	せきじゅう字	_____	_____

28. Correct either the reading or writing mistakes in the following words.

十方円	じゅうまんえん	新い	あたらしい	五寺半	ごじばん
高い	だかい	口分	よんぷん	昼	よる
牛後	ごご	羊分	はんぶん	今月	いまつき

Block 4: Lessons 16-20

RAKUJŌ － New vocabulary 新しい単語

どこ	where?	きっと	surely
出る	to go out (group 1)	会える	to be able to meet
戦う	to fight	話す	to speak
そうです	that's right	どうして	why?
勇気	courage, bravery	やめる	to stop, to abandon
出す	to take out	感動する	to be impressed
弾	bullet	条件	condition
ソルジャー (soldier)	soldier	伝える	to convey (group 1)
休戦	truce	聞く	to listen
将来	future	撤去する	to dismantle
攻める	to attack	再開する	to resume
チャンス (chance)	chance	よろしい	good, all right (formal)

1. Based on what you have read in the fourth chapter of *Rakujō*, what verbal form (simple or formal) does Yodo use when she speaks with Yasu? How about Yasu when he speaks with Yodo? Why do you think they use these verbal forms toward each other?

2. Explain why one of the fighting soldiers uses the verb いる in his sentence ここにいたか！？, whereas another soldier uses the verb ある in his sentence 弾がない！

3. Change Yuki's sentence ヨド様！ヤス様はここにいます。ヤス様と話しませんか？ into the simple form. Why does he use the formal form in this context?

4. Conjugate these two verbs into the different forms indicated.

話す	simple present affirmative	伝える
_____	simple past affirmative	_____
_____	simple present negative	_____
_____	simple past negative	_____
_____	formal present affirmative	_____
_____	formal past affirmative	_____
_____	formal present negative	_____
_____	formal past negative	_____

5. Say what the end-of-sentence particle の means in Yodo's sentence at the beginning of the chapter ユキはどこにいるの？

6. Say what the end-of-sentence particles よ and ぞ mean in the words uttered by Yuki before his soldiers 皆、勇気を出すよ！ 戦うぞ！

7. What function do the particles の and を have in the sentence 休戦の条件を伝えるぞ？

8. What function do the particles へ and と have in the sentence ユキ様は「外へ出ます」と言いました?

9. Place each word in the box below in the corresponding category.

animals						
vegetables						
fruit						
stationery	ボールペン					
cutlery						
stores						
weather						

~~ボールペン~~	フォーク	もも	はえ	かぼちゃ	りんご	きり
からす	本屋	八百屋	秋	はし	雪	皿
バナナ	くじら	たまねぎ	ナイフ	しか	くつ屋	肉屋
梅雨	ふで	ピーマン	パン屋	馬	紙	レタス
じゃがいも	コップ	あり	嵐	切手	すいか	みかん

10. Link each one of the following words with the most appropriate matching verb.

ベッド	飲む	日本語	教える
手紙	買う	ご飯	呼ぶ
ボール	起きる	本	食べる
お茶	書く	人	帰る
ケーキ屋	遊ぶ	家	書く

11. Which of the existence verbs, ある or いる, is the most appropriate in the following sentences? What meaning (to be, there is/are, to have) do they have in each case?

a) 私は車が___ある___。 (meaning: to have)

b) 外にかえるが二匹_____。 (meaning:)

c) ジョナサンくんは教室に_____。 (meaning:)

d) テーブルの上にめがねが_____。 (meaning:)

e) トモコちゃん、えんぴつが_____の？ (meaning:)

f) 庭に木が四本_____。 (meaning:)

12. Fill in the following sentences with the words in the box below.

a) 私は＿＿＿＿家＿＿＿＿へ帰る。

b) アキラくんとマヤちゃんは山へ＿＿＿＿＿＿＿＿。

c) 私はオレンジを＿＿＿＿＿＿＿＿。

d) テレビの上に＿＿＿＿＿＿＿＿がいる。

e) 彼女はコーヒーを＿＿＿＿＿＿＿＿。

f) ミツヒコさんは＿＿＿＿＿＿＿＿で＿＿＿＿＿＿＿＿を飲む。

g) 本田さんは本を＿＿＿＿＿＿＿＿。

h) テレビの上に＿＿＿＿＿＿＿＿がある。

読む　猫　行く　飲む　お金　スプーン　~~家~~　スープ　食べる

---

13. Change the verbs whose meaning doesn't fit in the following sentences with othe[r] verbs that fit in with the context.

a) 彼はなしを~~飲みます~~。 **食べます**
b) 犬はあそこになかった。

c) 私はざっしを食べた。
d) 車で東京へ買った

e) あの山に川はいません。
f) さめは海にない

g) あなたはきれいな漢字を急いだ。
h) 先生は私に日本語を遊びます。

14. Indicate the register of the following sentences (formal, colloquial, or vulgar), an[d] say, as well, whether the speaker is a man, a woman, or whether it could be both.

a) あそこにとらがいたぞ！　　　　　（　vulgar ｜ man　）

b) 青山さん、図書館へ行きますか？　（　　　　　　）

c) そうなの？へー、おもしろいわ。　（　　　　　　）

d) すみません、あれはオレの車だよ。（　　　　　　）

e) ここでは日本語を教えますね。　　（　　　　　　）

f) すしを食べなかったぜ！　　　　　（　　　　　　）

15. Choose the correct grammatical particle in each case.

a) これ____私____自転車です。

　　1.を　2.は　3.の　4.で

　　1.の　2.に　3.を　4.へ

b) アキオさんは明日<ruby>明日<rt>あした</rt></ruby>アメリカ____<ruby>行<rt>い</rt></ruby>く____<ruby>言<rt>い</rt></ruby>いました。

　　1.で　2.は　3.と　4.へ

　　1.に　2.と　3.は　4.を

c) マリコちゃんは<ruby>家<rt>いえ</rt></ruby>____<ruby>紙<rt>かみ</rt></ruby>____<ruby>漢字<rt>かんじ</rt></ruby>____<ruby>書<rt>か</rt></ruby>いた。

　　1.へ　2.に　3.で　4.が

　　1.へ　2.に　3.で　4.が

　　1.を　2.と　3.に　4.の

16. Complete the following sentences with the correct particles.

a) <ruby>先生<rt>せんせい</rt></ruby>____きれいな<ruby>教室<rt>きょうしつ</rt></ruby>____いました。

b) 今、<ruby>僕<rt>ぼく</rt></ruby>____<ruby>頭<rt>あたま</rt></ruby>____いたいです。

c) <ruby>先生<rt>せんせい</rt></ruby>____<ruby>学生<rt>がくせい</rt></ruby>____スペイン<ruby>語<rt>ご</rt></ruby>____<ruby>教<rt>おし</rt></ruby>えました。

d) <ruby>今日<rt>きょう</rt></ruby>は<ruby>病院<rt>びょういん</rt></ruby>____<ruby>自転車<rt>じてんしゃ</rt></ruby>____<ruby>行<rt>い</rt></ruby>く。

e) テーブルの上____えんぴつ____ボールペンがあります。

f) <ruby>三時間前<rt>さんじかんまえ</rt></ruby>、私は<ruby>彼女<rt>かのじょ</rt></ruby>____<ruby>手紙<rt>てがみ</rt></ruby>____<ruby>読<rt>よ</rt></ruby>んだ。

g) だれ____本____あげましたか？ | <ruby>高田<rt>たかだ</rt></ruby>さん____あげたよ。

h)「<ruby>君<rt>きみ</rt></ruby>、<ruby>家<rt>いえ</rt></ruby>____トモくん____<ruby>遊<rt>あそ</rt></ruby>ぶの？」____<ruby>彼<rt>かれ</rt></ruby>は<ruby>言<rt>い</rt></ruby>った。

17. Correct any grammatical particle mistakes in the following sentences.

a) 私と<ruby>名前<rt>なまえ</rt></ruby>はジョナサンです。

b) <ruby>彼女<rt>かのじょ</rt></ruby>は<ruby>家<rt>いえ</rt></ruby>でいる。しかし、<ruby>教室<rt>きょうしつ</rt></ruby>に<ruby>勉強<rt>べんきょう</rt></ruby>する。

c) フミコさんは<ruby>電車<rt>でんしゃ</rt></ruby>にここを<ruby>来<rt>き</rt></ruby>ますよ。

d) 私はレストランがケーキの<ruby>食<rt>た</rt></ruby>べる。

18. Complete the following table as in the example.

います	いました	いる	いた
いません	いませんでした	いない	いなかった
あります		ある	あった
	ありませんでした		
	食べました		食べた
食べません		食べない	
呼びます		呼ぶ	
	呼びませんでした		
			持った
持ちません		持たない	
		守る	

19. Arrange the following portions to form a correct sentence.

a) ここ｜います｜が｜あり｜に   <u>   ここにありがいます。   </u>

b) です｜車｜青い｜は｜の｜私   <u>   </u>

c) 庭｜遊んだ｜先生｜で｜と｜は｜私   <u>   </u>

d) りんご｜を｜あなた｜食べました｜か｜は   <u>   </u>

e) 私｜で｜へ｜電車｜帰る｜家｜は   <u>   </u>

f) 彼｜家｜か｜しずか(な)｜の｜は｜です   <u>   </u>

20. Correct any conjugation mistakes of the verbs in the following sentences.

a) あの鳥はケーキを食べないかった。

b) 二時間前、彼女の家へ行きます。

c) ここでやさいを買あない。

d) 明日、社長とコーヒーを飲まなかった。

見	行	来	帰	買	売	教	食	飲	持	待
(131)	(100)	(101)	(123)	(117)	(118)	(134)	(150)	(151)	(115)	(116)
思	出	入	上	下	右	左	中	外	間	石
(132)	(69)	(70)	(60)	(61)	(62)	(63)	(64)	(145)	(91)	(45)

21. Develop the stroke order of the following kanji.

来					
買					
食					
右					
待					

22. Link each kanji with its most common reading (usually, the *kun'yomi*).

見る	みぎ	外	おもう
右	みる	思う	くる
売る	はいる	買う	なか
入る	いし	来る	そと
石	うる	出る	でる
左	ひだり	中	かう

23. Indicate the correct kanji or kanji combination for each reading.

a) かえる

1.掃える　2.帰る　3.帰える　4.掃る

b) ばいしゅん

1.買春　2.買秋　3.売秋　4.売春

c) もつ

1.待つ　2.特つ　3.持つ　4.時つ

d) いんしょく

1.食飯　2.飲食　3.食飯　4.食飲

24. Indicate the correct reading for each kanji combination.

a) 来月、わたしの家<ruby>家<rt>いえ</rt></ruby>へ来ますか？

来月：1.らいげつ　2.らいがつ　3.くるつき　4.くつき

来ます：1.いきます　2.きます　3.くます　4.かえります

b) あの金持ちは大きい<ruby>教室<rt>きょうしつ</rt></ruby>に入った。

金持ち：1.かねまち　2.きんまち　3.かねもち　4.きんもち

入る：1.はった　2.いった　3.でった　4.はいった

c) 今、時間がない。後でその見本を<ruby>読<rt>よ</rt></ruby>みますよ。

時間：1.じかん　2.しかん　3.じがん　4.しがん

見本：1.みき　2.けんき　3.みほん　4.けんほん

25. Provide in hiragana the readings of the following words, and give their meaning. (**Note:** The words marked with an asterisk appear in kanji tables studied in previous blocks.)

出る	_____	_____	右	_____ _____
石	_____	_____	教える	_____ _____
行う	_____	_____	下がる	_____ _____
*人間	_____	_____	*朝食	_____ _____

26. Write the following words in kanji, and give their meanings.

うえ	_____	_____	なか	_____ _____
いく	_____	_____	あいだ	_____ _____
がいじん	_____	_____	おもう	_____ _____
*ちゅうねん	_____	_____	*やかん	_____ _____

27. Correct either the reading or writing mistakes in the following words.

待つ	もつ	下がる	あがる	飲む	なむ
左石	さゆう	時聞	じかん	貝る	みる
人る	はいる	買売	ばいばい	昼食	ちょうしょく

Block 5: Lessons 21-25

RAKUJŌ — New vocabulary 新しい単語

ひどい	terrible, cruel	もちろん	of course
頑固な （がんこ）	stubborn	深い （ふか）	deep
なる	to become	考える （かんが）	to think (group 1)
命令 （めいれい）	command	あやまる	to apologize (group 2)
従う （したが）	to follow, to obey	物 （もの）	thing (tangible)

1. Based on what you have read in chapter 5 of *Rakujō*, why does Yodo get so angry with Yasu, up to the point where she goes to speak with him and insults him? Make a list of the insults and swear words Yodo says in this chapter.

2. What does the word おじいさん literally mean? And, in the context where it appears in *Rakujō*, uttered by Yodo before Yasu, what meaning do you think it acquires?

3. How many cannons (inside and outside) were there at the Saka base before they were dismantled? What counter do we use to "count" these cannons? And, if they were trees instead of cannons, what counter would we use? And what if they were pigeons?

4. In this chapter there are three adverbs derived from adjectives. Specify them, and indicate what adjective they come from originally.

5. Transform into adverbs the adjectives ひどい, 頑固（がんこ）な and 遅（おそ）い.

6. What do the following adverbs mean: もう, だけ、少（すこ）し and とても?

7. In this chapter there are four verbs conjugated in the *-te* form. Specify them, and indicate, as well, their dictionary form (simple form), *-masu* form, and their meaning.

8. Conjugate the following verbs into each of the given forms.

あやまる (simple gerund):
従（したが）う (request):
負（ま）ける (formal negative gerund):
壊（こわ）す (simple past gerund):

9. In the text (of he 5ᵗʰ chapter) there are two *-suru* verbs. Specify them, and indicate their dictionary form (simple form), *-masu* form, *-te* form, and their meaning.

10. What word does Hide use to address his mother? Why does he use this word instead of 母（はは）?

11. Place each word in the list in its corresponding box for counters.

人 (にん)	兄						
枚 (まい)							
台 (だい)							
本 (ほん)							
匹 (ひき)							
頭 (とう)							
冊 (さつ)							
個 (こ)							

兄 (あに)	電車 (でんしゃ)	先生 (せんせい)	かえる	車 (くるま)	へび	マンガ
いちご	紙 (かみ)	羊 (ひつじ)	カメラ	くま	男	手紙 (てがみ)
足 (あし)	えんぴつ	本	ディスク	妻 (つま)	オレンジ	ぶた
バナナ	パソコン	あり	ふで	コンピュータ	自転車 (じてんしゃ)	ライオン
猫 (ねこ)	雑誌 (ざっし)	たこ	警察官 (けいさつかん)	新聞 (しんぶん)	さる	馬 (うま)
ボール	ゴム	おじいさん	木	もも	切手 (きって)	みかん
とら	母親 (ははおや)	象 (ぞう)	すし	バス	写真 (しゃしん)	ボールペン

12. Complete the following sentences with the most appropriate counter, and add the reading of the "counter + number" combination. Indicate their ~つ equivalent, as well.

a) あの人の家には車が(3)<u>三台</u>あります。   (三つ (みっ))

b) なしを(9)＿＿＿ください。   (・)

c) この建物は(8)＿＿＿あります。(何)＿＿＿に行きますか？   ( ) ( )

d) あなたは子供が(2)＿＿＿いますか？   ( )

e) 道には大きい牛が(4)＿＿＿いるぜ！   ( )

f) この(6)＿＿＿の本を読んだか？   ( )

g) 今日はビデオを(3)＿＿＿見ましたよ。   ( )

h) あそこに犬が(1)＿＿＿いたと思います。   ( )

13. Link each of the following words with its most suitable counterpart.

おかあさん	おねえさん	パパ	とうちゃん
おっと	だんなさん	おふくろ	つま
かない	はは	おばさん	おばあさん
むすめさん	おじいちゃん	あに	おば
あね	むすめ	にょうぼう	おにいさん
そふ	おくさん	そぼ	ははおや

14. Correct the use of vocabulary in the following sentences when necessary. (Bear in mind social positions.)

a) アキラの~~父~~お父さんはラーメン屋さんだ。

b) あたしの妹さんはとてもバカだよ。

c) 私のお母さんは昨日、ケーキを三つ食べたよ。

d) あなたの妻はたいへん美しいですね。

e) 石川さんのいとこは本を買いました。

15. Choose the most appropriate answer in each case.

a) _____、私は映画館へ行きました。

    1.まだ　2.あさって　3.明日　4.昨日

b) サオリちゃんの雑誌はつくえの_____あると思うよ。

    1.とても　2.上に　3.ゆっくり　4.やっぱり

c) このなすとかぼちゃを_____売ってくださいよ、八百屋さん！

    1.安く　2.低く　3.小さく　4.むずかしく

d) 中田先生は_____教室にいますよ。

    1.そばに　2.もっと　3.きっと　4.いくら

e) あの人は_____漢字を書いている。

    1.危険に　2.きらいに　3.ひまに　4.上手に

16. Complete the table by following the example. (**Note:** If you have any doubts about which group a verb belongs to, check Appendix ɪᴠ in the textbook.)

洗う	洗って	to wash	座る		
見る					to buy
		to sleep		抱いて	
	急いで		行く		
	貸して		作る		
		to play	ある		
呼ぶ					to read
疲れる				来て	
	して		走る		
飲む					to die
		to teach	歩く		
歌う			知る		

17. Complete the following sentences by conjugating the verb into the given form.

a) 今、彼の写真を___見ていました___。(見る | formal past gerund)

b) いいえ、映画はまだ＿＿＿＿＿＿＿。(終わる | informal negative gerund)

c) おもしろくないですか？＿＿＿＿＿＿＿よ！(笑う | request)

d) 青木くん！先生が＿＿＿＿＿＿＿よ。(呼ぶ | informal present gerund)

e) 明日、広島へ＿＿＿＿＿＿＿。(行く | request)

f) いいえ、私はあのかえるを＿＿＿＿＿＿＿。(殺す | formal negative gerund)

g) 西田先輩は今たばこを＿＿＿＿＿＿＿か？(吸う | formal present gerund)

h) あなたが大嫌いだ！家へ＿＿＿＿＿＿＿。(帰る | request)

i) 私？＿＿＿＿＿＿＿よ、酒。(飲む | formal past negative gerund)

18. Place each one of the adverbs from the box below in the corresponding space (**Note:** In the case of adjectives, you must transform them into adverbs first.)

a) あなた！うるさいですよ！____静かに____食べてくださいね。

b) A: 妹はどこにいるの？｜B: テレビの_____座っているよ！

c) 明日、もっと_____来てください！わかったか？

d) _____、彼は来なかった。しかし、_____は来ると思うよ。

e) 彼女は_____来ますよ。_____待ってくださいね。

f) トモコちゃん！この字は大きいよ！_____書いてね。

g) あの人は_____歌いました。

昨日　前に　小さい　きっと　~~静かな~~　早い　上手な　ちょっと　明日

---

19. The nouns in parentheses can become -*suru* verbs. Transform them into verbs, and then conjugate each of them into the given forms.

a) アサミさんにこれをすると____約束した____。（約束｜informal past）

b) あの女は山本さんと_____よ。（結婚｜formal past gerund）

c) ユズヒコ！テレビを見るな！_____よ！（勉強｜request）

d) オサムくんは車を_____。（運転｜formal gerund）

e) バスはまだ_____。（出発｜informal past negative）

20. Complete the following sentences with the correct particles.

a) モモコさん____自転車は大学の前____ある____思います。

b) A: 学校____バス____来ますか？B: いいえ、電車____来ますよ。

c) 彼女____教室____お母さん____ケーキ____食べているか？

d) 姉____弟は私に映画____好きだ____言っている。

e) ここ____は私____本____2冊あります。本田さん____あげてください。

父	母	弟	兄	姉	妹	多	少	休	体	力
(36)	(37)	(38)	(39)	(40)	(41)	(51)	(52)	(124)	(125)	(108)
名	元	気	家	会	社	近	遠	広	強	弱
(102)	(66)	(67)	(160)	(80)	(81)	(96)	(97)	(111)	(106)	(107)

21. Develop the stroke order of the following kanji.

弟					
姉					
気					
弱					
家					

22. Link each kanji with its most common reading (usually, the *kun'yomi*).

父   いもうと   体   からだ
妹   おとうと   弱い   つよい
近い   おおい   強い   よわい
遠い   ちかい   家   いえ
弟   とおい   兄   あね
多い   ちち   姉   あに

23. Indicate the correct kanji or kanji combination for each reading.

a) ひろい

  1.広い   2.遠い   3.多い   4.弱い

b) あね

  1.兄   2.弟   3.姉   4.妹

c) かいしゃ

  1.今社   2.社今   3.社会   4.会社

d) ふぼ

  1.父母   2.祖父   3.母父   4.祖母

24. Indicate the correct reading for each kanji combination.

a) あの<u>少年</u>の<u>名前</u>はなんですか？

　少年：1.しょうとし　2.しょうねん　3.しゅうねん　4.しゅうとし

　名前：1.めいぜん　2.まなえ　3.めいまえ　4.なまえ

b) お<u>父</u>さんはバルセロナと神戸(こうべ)が<u>姉妹</u>都市(とし)だと言(い)いました。

　父：　1.ちち　2.かあ　3.はは　4.とう

　姉妹：1.あねいもうと　2.いもうとあね　3.しまい　4.まいし

c) オレのバカ<u>弟</u>は<u>元気</u>にマンガ<u>家</u>になりたいと言(い)っているぞ！

　弟：　1.おとうと　2.いもうと　3.あね　4.あに

　元気：1.きげん　2.もとき　3.げんき　4.きもと

　家：　1.か　2.け　3.いえ　4.うち

25. Give the reading in *furigana* of the underlined kanji.

a)　<u>会社</u>へ行く前に、彼女(かのじょ)に<u>会</u>いました。

b)　昨日(きのう)は<u>天気</u>がよかったですね。ちょっと<u>家</u>を出て、<u>遠</u>くへ行った。

c)　おい！「<u>社会</u>の窓(まど)」が<u>開</u>(あ)いてるよ、お<u>兄</u>さん！(**Note.** 社会の窓(まど) ＝ the "fly")

d)　<u>体力</u>がないね...私の<u>体</u>は<u>少</u>し<u>弱</u>いと思う...<u>休</u>むな！

26. Write the following words in kanji, and give their meaning. (**Note:** The words marked with an asterisk appear in kanji tables studied in previous blocks.)

はは	_____	_____	ちから	_____	_____
ひろい	_____	_____	つよい	_____	_____
きゅうじつ	_____	_____	たぶん	_____	_____
*にんき	_____	_____	*きもち	_____	_____

27. Correct either the reading or writing mistakes in the following words.

柿	あね	気待ち	きもち	休力	たいりょく
広大	ひろおお	人気	じんき	会社	しゃかい
小年	しょうねん	刀強い	ちからづよい	第	おとんと

銀河350年9月6日に、サカ基地が落城した。
ユキ、ヨドとヒデのアーミーが全滅した。ヤスは銀河の独裁者になった。
しかし、サカ基地のソルジャーの勇気は今も皆覚えている。

Block 6: Lessons 26-30

RAKUJŌ — New vocabulary 新しい単語

だまる	to be quiet	やろう	guy, fellow
気持ち	feeling	負け犬	loser, underdog
悲しい	sad	落城する	to fall (a castle)
すぐ	at once	全滅する	to be annihilated
許す	to forgive, to allow	独裁者	dictator
合戦する	to battle	覚える	to remember (group 1)

1. Based on what you have read in the sixth chapter of *Rakujō*, why does Hide use the expression ただいま in the first panel? How does the soldier inside reply to this?

2. What expression would Hide use if he entered, for example, Yasu's house? How would Yasu (being at home) reply to him?

3. According to Yodo's remark, what part of her body is hurting? In addition to answering the question, write the sentences "My back hurts," "I have an earache," and "my knee hurts" in Japanese.

4. In this chapter there are three onomatopoeic expressions used in the dialogue. Find them and specify in each case whether they are *giongo* or *gitaigo*.

5. What does the expression 悲^{かな}しくなる mean? Use the verb なる with the words 便利^{べんり}な, 深^{ふか}い and リーダー, and give the meaning of the resulting expression.

6. In Hide's sentence 「ユキ、母と話^{はな}しにいってあげてください。とても悲^{かな}しくなったよ。行ってくれる？」, what nuance do the verbs あげる and くれる add?

7. Conjugate the following verbs into the given imperative forms.

	"Rough" imperative	*-nasai* imperative
呼^よぶ	_____	_____
だまる	_____	_____
許^{ゆる}す	_____	_____
待つ	_____	_____
覚^{おぼ}える	_____	_____

8. In the text we find the sentence 呼^よびにいきます. What is its meaning? Transform the verbs in the previous exercise into this ~にいきます form.

9. What is the meaning of the set phrases 頭^{あたま}がいい and 腕^{うで}がいい? (If your *Japanese in MangaLand* edition is either the 1st or the 2nd one, check page 94 of this workbook.)

第六部

10. Place each word from the list below in its corresponding box.

Head	ひたい						
Torso							
Limbs							
Hand							

~~ひたい~~	ひじ	め 目	なかゆび 中指	ひとさ ゆび 人差し指	つめ 爪	した 舌
てくび 手首	あし 足	ひげ	て ひら 手の平	あしもと 足元	け かみの毛	こゆび 小指
あたま 頭	ゆび 指	おなか	のど	くち 口	まつげ	あご
ほお	て 手	ひざ	むね 胸	かお 顔	せなか 背中	かた 肩
へそ	くび 首	は 歯	みみ 耳	はな 鼻	うで	おやゆび 親指

11. Link each of the situations stated below with the most suitable expression of daily life.

たんじょうび
1. 誕生日

2. 私は私の家に入る

や　　みせ　い
3. 本屋さんに入る。店の人はこう言う

い
4. 私の家を出る。母はこう言う

はん
5. ご飯を食べる前

せんせい
6. 私は先生の家に入る

7. 1月1日

8. ごめんなさい

はん
9. ご飯を食べた後

しけん　　ごうかく
10. 試験に合格した！

しごと　お　　　　かちょう　い
11. 仕事を終わった。課長はこう言う

あ
a. 明けましておめでとうございます！

b. いらっしゃいませ！

さま
c. ごちそう様でした

もう　わけ
d. 申し訳ありません

たんじょうび
e. 誕生日おめでとうございます！

つか　さま
f. お疲れ様です

g. いってらっしゃい

h. おめでとうございます！

i. ただいま

じゃま
j. お邪魔します

k. いただきます！

Extra vocabulary: 誕生日: birthday | 店: store | こう: thus, so | 合格する: to pass an exam

12. Choose the most appropriate answer in each case.

a) ヒデキさんは＿＿＿＿＿と笑_{わら}いましたよ。

    1.くたくた　2.げらげら　3.ぴかぴか　4.わくわく

b) 今日_{きょう}は彼女_{かのじょ}のお母さんとお父さんに会う。＿＿＿＿＿するね！

    1.げらげら　2.しくしく　3.ぱくぱく　4.どきどき

c) ああ！トイレに行った！＿＿＿＿＿したぞ！

    1.すっきり　2.しっかり　3.ぐるぐる　4.いらいら

d) お腹_{なか}が＿＿＿＿＿だ。レストランへ行って、＿＿＿＿＿食べるぞ！

    1.ぺこぺこ　2.ぺらぺら　3.からから　4.いらいら

    1.くたくた　2.しくしく　3.ぱくぱく　4.わくわく

13. Place each of the words from the box below into the corresponding space.

a)　私の名前はフォスターです。＿＿＿＿＿＿＿＿。

b)　彼女_{かのじょ}の黒_{くろ}い＿＿＿＿＿＿＿＿はとても長_{なが}いです。

c)　マキコちゃんは＿＿＿＿＿＿＿＿泣_ないている。

d)　私のお父さんの兄は私の＿＿＿＿＿＿＿＿です。

e)　家の前に＿＿＿＿＿＿＿＿が一頭_{いっとう}いますよ！

f)　あたしの＿＿＿＿＿＿＿＿はとてもかっこいいですわ！ほほほ！

g)　トムさんは＿＿＿＿＿＿＿＿が青いですね。

h)　ツネオのお父さんの母はツネオの＿＿＿＿＿＿＿＿です。

i)　ノボル: ただいま！｜お母さん: あ、ノボル、＿＿＿＿＿＿＿＿！

j)　家の前に＿＿＿＿＿＿＿＿が一匹_{いっぴき}いますよ！

k)　＿＿＿＿＿＿＿＿がすいたよ！

l)　私の母の母は私の＿＿＿＿＿＿＿＿です。

m)　指輪_{ゆびわ}をもらったので、＿＿＿＿＿＿＿＿にはめた。

n)　あの人は、日本語_ごが＿＿＿＿＿＿＿＿ですね！すごいわ！

おじ　祖母_{そぼ}　よろしくお願_{ねが}いします　ぺらぺら　さる　おばあさん
薬指_{くすりゆび}　かみの毛_け　だんな　馬_{うま}　おかえりなさい　お腹_{なか}　しくしく　目_め

14. Complete the table following the example. (**Note:** If you have any doubts about which group a verbs belongs to, check Appendix IV in the textbook.)

食(た)べろ	食(た)べなさい	食(た)べてくれ	食(た)べるな	to eat
行け				
	回(まわ)りなさい			
読(よ)め				
		貸(か)してくれ		
			触(さわ)るな	
洗(あら)え				
	教えなさい			
		呼(よ)んでくれ		
			狙(ねら)うな	
	死(し)になさい			
			走(はし)るな	
急(いそ)げ				

15. Specify in the table who gives and who receives the objects or actions exchanged in the following sentences.

a) 私はエリカさんにボールペンをあげた。

b) アケミさんは私にパソコンをくれました。

c) 弟はお母さんに手紙(てがみ)を書(か)いてあげた。

d) クミちゃんはテツさんに自転車(じてんしゃ)をもらいます。

e) 山本(やまもと)くん、これをモモコさんにあげてください。

f) 私は学生(がくせい)に本屋(や)さんに行ってもらった。

g) 兄は山田(やまだ)さんにおもしろい雑誌(ざっし)をもらいました。

	Gives	Receives
	私	エリカ

16. Place each one of the words in parentheses into the following sentences. Don't forget to conjugate them or to make the appropriate grammatical changes.

a) 川田さんは二年前＿＿先生に＿＿なった。 （先生）

b) 昨日、課長の家へ＿＿＿＿＿＿＿に行きました。 （遊ぶ）

c) 私はすしがとても＿＿＿＿＿＿＿なった。 （好きな）

d) あの人はとても腕が＿＿＿＿＿＿なりましたね。 （いい）

e) 本田くん、これを＿＿＿＿＿＿来てくれますか？ （読む）

17. Indicate the most appropriate answer in each case.

a) キヨコ！皿を＿＿＿＿＿よ！
　　1.洗い　2.洗いさい　3.洗え　4.洗お

b) ヒロシ！魚屋さんへ魚を＿＿＿＿＿に行ってくれますか？
　　1.買い　2.買え　3.買う　4.買って

c) あの人は「あそこへ電車＿＿＿＿＿行ってくれ」と言ったよ。
　　1.に　2.と　3.は　4.で

d) 金田さんは私にＣＤを＿＿＿＿＿。
　　1.もらえ　2.あげなさい　3.くれました　4.あげた

e) ヨーコ！ここへ＿＿＿＿＿よ！
　　1.来なさい　2.来なさい　3.来なさい　4.来なさい

f) ＿＿＿＿＿お風呂に入りなさいよ！
　　1.早い　2.速い　3.早く　4.速く

g) アキラ！ここへ＿＿＿＿＿！
　　1.来い　2.来い　3.来い　4.来い

h) 今日は耳＿＿＿＿＿とても痛いぞ！
　　1.と　2.が　3.は　4.を

i) おい、君！オレの彼女をじっと＿＿＿＿＿！殺すぞ！
　　1.見なさい　2.見ろ　3.見てください　4.見るな

口	目	手	足	心	耳	店	学	校	先	生
(23)	(24)	(25)	(26)	(27)	(28)	(75)	(76)	(77)	(78)	(79)
楽	変	国	語	言	立	道	車	自	友	文
(157)	(147)	(152)	(153)	(126)	(109)	(92)	(93)	(94)	(103)	(68)

18. Develop the stroke order of the following kanji.

足					
学					
先					
国					
車					

19. Link each kanji with its most common reading (usually, the *kun'yomi*).

国	くち	目	なま
口	みみ	変	め
心	こころ	生	みせ
足	くに	道	て
車	くるま	手	みち
耳	あし	店	へん

20. Indicate the correct kanji or kanji combination for each reading.

a) たのしい
 1.楽しい　2.薬しい　3.楽い　4.薬い

b) がくせい
 1.先生　2.学生　3.生先　4.生学

c) がっこう
 1.学年　2.学国　3.学校　4.学生

d) がいこく
 1.入国　2.国入　3.外国　4.国外

21. Indicate the correct reading for each kanji combination.

a) 今日、大学へ行った。友だちと先生に会った。
きょう

　大学：1.だいかく　2.たいかく　3.だいがく　4.たいがく

　友だち：1.どもだち　2.ゆだち　3.ゆうだち　4.ともだち

　先生：1.せいせん　2.せえせん　3.せんせい　4.せんせえ

b) あなたは中国語ができますか？よかった、安心しましたよ。

　中国語：1.ちゅこくご　2.ちゅうごくこ　3.ちゅごくご　4.ちゅうごくご

　安心：1.やすごころ　2.あんしん　3.やすこころ　4.あんじん

c) A: あの高校生を殺したか？ | B: いいえ、まだ生きているぞ！
ころ

　高校生：1.こうこうせい　2.ここせい　3.こうこせい　4.ここうせい

　生きている：1.なまきている　2.いきている　3.うきている　4.せいきている

22. Give the reading in *furigana* of the underlined kanji.

a)　先月の遠足は楽しかったね！

b)　出口の売店へ先に行ってください。その前の道に車があります。

c)　お前はあの私立学校の中学生を殺したの？早く自白してくれ！

d)　赤道へ行く楽な近道を言ってください。

23. Write the following words in kanji, and give their meaning. (**Note:** The words marked with an asterisk appear in kanji tables studied in previous blocks.)

くち	_____ _____	みみ	_____ _____
あし	_____ _____	じんせい	_____ _____
たのしい	_____ _____	にほんご	_____ _____
*ぼこく	_____ _____	*ぶんめい	_____ _____

24. Correct either the reading or writing mistakes in the following words.

赤わる	かわる	生月	せんげつ	毛足	てあじ
学なぶ	まなぶ	立つ	てつ	犬変	たいへん
仲心	ちゅうしん	目分	じぶん	人口	いりぐち

Appendix: Answers to the exercises

Here you will find the answers to all exercises in this book, and so that you can check whether you have solved them correctly. However, as we cautioned you in the textbook, remember that you should first do the exercises, and then check the answers. Don't read this section before you have finished an exercise, because it would be completely counterproductive, and this book of supplementary exercises would lose all reason to exist regarding your learning. It is also important to mention that, although we have tried to take into account all variables, there can sometimes be more than one correct answer or more than one possibility. Don't take these answers as definitive, but as a flexible guide so that you can determine whether or not you have grasped the grammatical concepts presented in each lesson. Therefore, some of your own creative answers may be correct.

Block 1

1. カッカッカッカッ: footsteps | わははははは: boisterous laugh | ゴゴゴゴ: sound of a plane or a spaceship flying | ドカーーン: explosion | ガキィィィン: swords clashing | ひゅ ——: a flying object rents the air at full speed.

2. ユキ.

3. 1st army: 89,354 men | 3rd army: 150,321 men.

4. 1st: はちまんきゅうせんさんびゃくごじゅうよん | 2nd: じゅうにまんさんぜんろっぴゃくにじゅうはち | 3rd: じゅうごまんさんびゃくにじゅういち.

5. b) 1. おやすみなさい | c) 3. おめでとうございます | d) 1. またね！ e) 2. はい、元気です.

6. To a friend you would probably answer いいえ. To a stranger, the most appropriate would be どういたしまして.

7. The literal meaning is "take care of your spirit," although it is very often used to say goodbye, with the meaning of "take care."

8. You: おはようございます. | Storekeeper: いらっしゃいませ. | You: これはいくらですか？

Storekeeper: これは 3　4　3 円です | You: 3　8　3 円ですか？ | Storekeeper:
いいえ、3　4　3 円です | You: これをお願いします (or これをください). | Store-
keeper: ありがとうございます. | You: どういたしまして (or いいえ). | Storekeeper: さよう
なら. | You: さようなら.

9. (Check on pages 24 and 25 of the textbook.)

10. の: no | き: ki | く: ku | さ: sa | じ: ji | し: shi | み: mi | ぱ: pa || ちゃ: cha | ぺ: pe | じょ:
jo | づ: zu | わ: wa | が: ga | ず: zu | ね: ne.

11. い: i | う: u | じゅ: ju | to: と | be: べ | chu: ちゅ || ぞ: zo | な: na | ちゃ: cha | o: お | go:
ご | rya: りゃ || ほ: po | ぬ: nu | りょ: ryo | pe: ぺ | wa: わ | gyu: ぎゅ || か: ka | を: (w)o | きゃ:
kya | ru: る | zu: ず or づ | ja: じゃ || り: ri | ん: n | みゅ: myu | mo: も | shi: し | byo: びょ.

12. おんがく: ongaku | いちご: ichigo | つなみ: tsunami || さかな: sakana | ちゃのゆ:
chanoyu | でんしゃ: densha || りょかん: ryokan | いしばし: ishibashi | くいだおれ:
kuidaore || いいわけ: iiwake | けいさつかん: keisatsukan | ふつかよい: futsukayoi ||
したぎ: shitagi | いきじごく: ikijigoku | かみのけ: kaminoke || どろぼう: dorobō | とう
きょう: tōkyō | きっぱり: kippari || くうしゅう: kūshū | ぎょうざ: gyōza | まっちゃ:
maccha || がんりゅう: ganryū | さっぽろ: sapporo | きょうみ: kyōmi || したっぱ: shitap-
pa | ぎゅうにゅう: gyūnyū | いろっぽい: iroppoi.

13. nihongo: にほんご | meitantei: めいたんてい | jitabata: じたばた || shamisen: しゃみ
せん | nemawashi: ねまわし | kannushi: かんぬし || nagoyaka: なごやか | tsuyu: つゆ |
tabako: たばこ || tanpopo: たんぽぽ | pakuri: ぱくり | ebisu: えびす || momiage: もみあげ
| tebukuro: てぶくろ | donzoko: どんぞこ || kyūri: きゅうり | jakkan: じゃっかん | assari:
あっさり || jūdō: じゅうどう | kenkyū: けんきゅう | buchō: ぶちょう || gunyagunya:
ぐにゃぐにゃ | kyūshū: きゅうしゅう | yappari: やっぱり || kyakka: きゃっか | nyōi:
にょうい | kyūdō: きゅうどう.

14. かがや: kagaya | おのはら: onohara | あっぱれ: appare || こっぱ: koppa | さぼてん:
saboten | はだか: hadaka || ぶらり: burari | こわっぱ: kowappa | うねりごえ: unerigoe ||
りょうつう: ryōtsū | のうぎょう: nōgyō | まみれ: mamire.

15. (Check on pages 32 and 33 of the textbook.)

16. デ: de | オ: o | ソ: so | マ: ma | ン: n | ム: mu | ゾ: zo | ア: a || チャ: cha | ジ: ji | プ: pu
| ミョ: myo | ス: su | ロ: ro | シュ: shu | レ: re.

解答

17. カ: ka | エ: e | ギョ: gyo | ze: ゼ | no: ノ | pyu: ピュ ‖ ド: do | ワ: wa | リャ: rya | u: ウ | n: ン | ja: ジャ ‖ ツ: tsu | フ: fu | チャ: cha | ke: ケ | wa: ワ | myo: ミョ ‖ メ: me | ク: ku | ピョ: pyo | ji: ジ or ヂ | yu: ユ | byu: ビュ ‖ ル: ru | ボ: po | ジョ: jo | bi: ビ | mi: ミ | sho: ショ.

18. パンダ: panda (panda) | ミルク: miruku (milk) | ワシントン: washinton (Washington) ‖ ロリコン: rorikon (Loli(ta) com(plex)) | ピアノ: piano (piano) | ゼネラル: zeneraru (general) ‖ ギャル: gyaru (girl) | ジャンボ: janbo (jumbo) | タンゴ: tango (tango) ‖ ララソン: marason (marathon) | ギリシア: girishia (Gresia) | ソンシツ: sonshitsu (損失) ‖ オランダ: oranda (Oranda) | シャワー: shawaa (shower) | ギブアップ: gibuappu (give up) ‖ キャラバン: kyaraban (caravan) | クリーナー: kuriinaa (cleener) | ハーモニー: haamonii (harmony) ‖ バグダッド: bagudaddo (Baghdad) | ルノアール: runoaaru (Renoir) | フットボール: futtobōru (football) ‖ キューピッド: kyūpiddo (Cupid) | マトリックス: matorikkusu (matrix) | チャーミング: chaamingu (charming) ‖ マスコット: masukotto (mascot) | アットマーク: attomaaku (at mark) | ホットポット: hottopotto (hot pot).

19. furansu: フランス (France) | shatsu: シャツ (shirt) | gurume: グルメ (gourmet) ‖ pasokon: パソコン (perso(nal) com(puter)) | arabama: アラバマ (Alabama) | igirisu: イギリス (English) ‖ maiwaifu: マイワイフ (my wife) | neruson: ネルソン (Nelson) | myunhen: ミュンヘン (Munchen) ‖ remon: レモン (lemon) | kyaria: キャリア (career) | napori: ナポリ (Napoli) ‖ nūdo: ヌード (nude) | apaato: アパート (apart(ment)) | gyappu: ギャップ (gap) ‖ kōhii: コーヒー (koffie) | kūdetaa: クーデター (coup d'etat) | raamen: ラーメン (lamian) ‖ pureeyaa: プレーヤー (player) | kukkii: クッキー (cookie) | piramiddo: ピラミッド (pyramid) ‖ chachacha: チャチャチャ (cha cha cha) | biitoruzu: ビートルズ (Beetles) | kyasshu: キャッシュ (cash) ‖ supittsu: スピッツ (spitz) | jaanarisuto: ジャーナリスト (journalist) | doraiyaa: ドライヤー (dryer).

20. シューマイ: shūmai (shao mai) | ソナタ: sonata (sonata) | レバー: rebaa (liver) ‖ ミスター: misutaa (mister) | アンドラ: andora (Andorra) | メキシコ: mekishiko (Mexico) ‖ ノウハウ: nouhau (know how) | ケース: keesu (case) | キャンセル: kyanseru (cancel) ‖ ビッグマン: bigguman (big man) | サッカー: sakkaa (soccer) | ナニワ: naniwa (浪速).

21. (Check the answer using the Compilation of Kanji in the textbook.)

22. 東: East | 六: six | 万: ten thousand | 円: yen | 南: South | 一: one ‖ 百: a hundred | 九: nine | 西: West | 北: North | 二: two | 十: ten.

23. 北: きた | 七: なな | 千: せん | 東: ひがし | 五: ご | 一: いち | 円: えん ‖ 十: じゅう | 三: さん | 西: にし | 万: まん | 南: みなみ | 八: はち.

24. 8: 八 (はち) | 3: 三 (さん) | 9: 九 or 九 (きゅう・く) ‖ 16: 十六 (じゅうろく) | 12: 十二 (じゅうに) | 24: 二十四 (にじゅうよん) ‖ 35: 三十五 (さんじゅうご) | 47: 四十七 (よんじゅうなな) | 50: 五十 (ごじゅう) ‖ 88: 八十八 (はちじゅうはち) | 111: 百十一 (ひゃくじゅういち) | 897: 八百九十七 (はっぴゃくきゅうじゅうなな) ‖ 7,200: 七千二百 (ななせんにひゃく) | 3,874: 三千八百七十四 (さんぜんはっぴゃくななじゅうよん) | 1,011: 千十一 (せんじゅういち).

25. 三: さん (3) | 五: ご (5) | 十九: じゅうきゅう or じゅうく (19) | 八十: はちじゅう (80) | 五十八: ごじゅうはち (58) | 九十五: きゅうじゅうご (95) | 百二: ひゃくに (102) | 三百五十七: さんびゃくごじゅうなな

(357)｜八千五十一：はっせんごじゅういち (8,051)｜千二百三十三：せんにひゃくさんじゅうさん (1,233)

26. 3,783: 三千七百八十三 <ruby>三千七百八十三<rt>さんぜんななひゃくはちじゅうさん</rt></ruby> ｜ 10,940: <ruby>一万九百四十<rt>いちまんきゅうひゃくよんじゅう</rt></ruby> ｜ 24,851: <ruby>二万四千八百五十<rt>にまんよんせんはっぴゃくごじゅう</rt></ruby>
<ruby>一<rt>いち</rt></ruby> ｜ 300,340: <ruby>三十万三百四十<rt>さんじゅうまんさんびゃくよんじゅう</rt></ruby> ｜ 834,901: <ruby>八十三万四千九百一<rt>はちじゅうさんまんよんせんきゅうひゃくいち</rt></ruby> ｜ 108,234: <ruby>十万八<rt>じゅうまんはっ</rt></ruby>
<ruby>千二百三十四<rt>せんにひゃくさんじゅうよん</rt></ruby> ｜ 560,205: <ruby>五十六万二百五<rt>ごじゅうろくまんにひゃくご</rt></ruby> ｜ 1,280,785: <ruby>百二十八万七百八十五<rt>ひゃくにじゅうはちまんななひゃくはちじゅうご</rt></ruby> ｜
75,034,026: <ruby>七千五百三万四千二十六<rt>ななせんごひゃくさんまんよんせんにじゅうろく</rt></ruby>｜834,201,016: <ruby>八億三千四百二十万千十六<rt>はちおくさんぜんよんひゃくにじゅうまんせんじゅうろく</rt></ruby>.

27. 五万七百二十九：ごまんななひゃくにじゅうきゅう (50,729) ｜ 十八万五千五百三十二：じゅうはちまんごせんごひゃくさんじゅうに (185,532) ｜ 三百八十七万五千二百十四：さんびゃくはちじゅうななまんごせんにひゃくじゅうよん (3,875,214) ｜ 二億三千二百万五千百十二：におくさんぜんにひゃくまんごせんひゃくじゅうに (232,005,112).

Block 2

1. If, according to the footnote, 銀河１年 is equivalent to the year 2153, the year 銀河３５０年 is 2153 + 349 = 2502.

2. <ruby>雨<rt>あめ</rt></ruby>です.

3. "Today" is ９月６日, therefore, in four days time, ９月１０日, there will be a 台風 "typhoon," according to Yuki.

4. Hide uses きみ to talk to Yuki, whereas Yodo uses おまえ. They are both hierarchically superior to Yuki and that is why they use these pronouns. In Yodo's case, since she is of a high social standing, with a domineering personality, it's normal that she uses the pronoun おまえ, which indicates she considers Yuki a very inferior subordinate. Hide, on the other hand, uses きみ, which doesn't have such a strong connotation in this context, still being a "pronoun used by a superior to talk to an inferior."

5. He conjugates です in its simple form, because he considers Yuki an inferior.

6. Hide's sentence is in the past negative. // Simple pres.: ライフルだ ｜ Simple past: ライフルだった ｜ Formal past: ライフルでした ｜ Simple neg.: ライフルではない ｜ Simple neg. (2): ライフルじゃない ｜ Formal neg.: ライフルではありません ｜ Simple past neg.: ライフルではなかった ｜ Simple past neg. (2): ライフルじゃなかった ｜ Formal past neg.: ライフルではありませんでした ｜ Formal past neg. (2): ライフルじゃありませんでした.

7. Yuki's answer: いいえ、ライフルではありませんでした. In the simple interrogative: ライフルではなかったか？ (or ライフルじゃなかったか？). In the formal interrogative:

ライフルではありませんでしたか？

8. cybot: サイボット ｜ shake: シェイク ｜ cybernet: サイバーネット ｜ fake: フェイク ｜ scandal: スキャンダル ｜ Venus: ビーナス or ヴィーナス ｜ ham: ハム ｜ guerrilla: ゲリラ, ゲリーヤ or ゲリリャ ｜ check: チェック ｜ tiramisu: ティラミス.

9. 4th of April: ４月４日 ｜ 12th of June: ６月１２日 ｜ 10th of August: ８月１０日 ｜ 6th of May: ５月６日 ｜ 26th of January: １月２６日 ｜ 17th of July: ７月１７日 ｜ 1st of December: １２月１日 ｜ 20th of September: ９月２０日 ｜ 24th of February: ２月２４日.

10. 昭和３０年: 1955 ｜ 明治５年: 1872 ｜ 平成２年: 1990 ｜ 大正１０年: 1921 ｜ 昭和５１年: 1976.

11. 夏: 暑い ｜ ６月: 梅雨 ｜ 春: 桜 ｜ 北海道: 雪 ‖ 涼しい: ３月 ｜ 秋: 紅葉 ｜ 暖かい: 沖縄 ｜ 冬: 寒い.

12. 1st person singular: 私, 僕, わし ｜ 1st person plural: 俺たち, われわれ ｜ 2nd person singular: あなた, 君, お前 ｜ 2nd person plural: お前ら, あんたたち.

13. 東京は嵐です (also 横浜, さいたま and 川崎) ｜ 沖縄は晴れではありません (also くもり) ｜ 九州は晴れです ｜ 名古屋はくもりです ｜ 仙台はくもりです ｜ 北海道は雨です ｜ 広島はくもりではありません (also 雨).

14. Sylvia: シルビア ｜ California: カリフォルニア ｜ George: ジョージ ｜ Chuck: チャック ｜ Dionysus: ディオニソス ｜ Constantinople: コンスタンチノープル ｜ Stephanie: ステファニー ｜ Canyon: キャニョン ｜ Jodie: ジョディー.

15. a) ２．それ ｜ b) １．あそこ ｜ c) ４．どこ ｜ d) １．あれ.

16. b) あれ ｜ c) ここ ｜ d) そこ ｜ e) どの ｜ f) この.

17. b) ではありません／じゃありません ｜ c) ですか？ ｜ d) ではない／じゃない ｜ e) ではありませんか？／じゃありませんか？ ｜ f) だった ｜ g) ではなかった／じゃなかった ｜ h) でしたか？

18. c) ７日 or 木曜日 ｜ d) ９日 ｜ e) 東京 ｜ f) (五日) ローマ ｜ g) (四日) ではありません ｜ h) (九日) 上海 ｜ i) (八日) any day of the week, except for 金曜日; or any city, except for アムステルダム will do.

19. b) われわれ ｜ c) 拙者 ｜ d) 君 ｜ e) 彼女 ｜ f) 俺ら ｜ g) 彼ら.

20. (Check the answer using the Compilation of Kanji in the textbook.)

21. 冬: ふゆ ｜ 本: ほん ｜ 男: おとこ ｜ 田: た ｜ 木: き ｜ 日: ひ ‖ 人: ひと ｜ 秋: あき ｜ 夏: なつ ｜ 火: ひ ｜ 子: こ ｜ 川: かわ.

22. a) 1.春 | b) 3.月 | c) 2.男女 | d) 4.私.

23. a) 4.もくようび | b) 2.にっぽんじん | c) 3.あまみず.

24. 秋:あき fall | 山:やま mountain | (平成)3年:さんねん year 3 of Heisei = 1991 | 女子:じょし girl | 水曜日:すいようび Wednesday | 春休み:はるやすみ spring vacation | 六日:むいか the sixth | 冬眠:とうみん hibernation | 油田:ゆでん oilfield.

25. おんな:女 woman | つき:月 moon | かわ:川 river | あめ:雨 rain | か曜日:火曜日 Tuesday | しがつ:四月 April | わたし:私 I | はつか:二十日 the 20ᵗʰ | ごねん:五年 5 years.

26. 日本 にほん | 年金 ねんきん | 土曜日 どようび | 冬休み ふゆやすみ | 金曜日 きんようび | 月曜日 げつようび | 火山 かざん | 女子 じょし.

Block 3

1. Yasu uses the suffix さん to talk to Yodo. He uses it as a sign of moderate respect. Using another suffix would mean excessively raising or lowering Yodo's standing.

2. Yodo uses 様 (さま) to talk to Yasu. It's a very formal suffix, indicating Yodo really respects Yasu, either due to his age or his social standing. This reveals Yodo is, to some extent, "subjugated" by Yasu. To talk about Hide, Yasu uses くん, a suffix used by a superior when talking to an inferior, especially if he is a boy. Therefore, Yasu, believes Hide has little influence, although he does show him some respect (otherwise, he would call him by his name alone).

3. It takes place at half past three in the afternoon. Either 午後三時半 (ごごさんじはん) or 十五時三十分 (じゅうごじさんじゅうぷん). / Yasu says he will return tomorrow at 2:45 (二時四十五分, にじよんじゅうごふん). An alternative way of saying the same time would be: 三時十五分前 (さんじじゅうごふんまえ).

4. -*i* adjectives: 忙しい (いそが), 美しい (うつく), みにくい, いい, 強い (つよ) | -*na* adjectives: 元気な (げんき), きれいな, 大切な (たいせつ), 無理な (むり), 大丈夫な (だいじょうぶ).

5. みにくいです | みにくい | みにくかったです | みにくかった | みにくくないです | みにくくない | みにくくなかったです | みにくくなかった ‖ きれいです | きれいだ | きれいでした | きれいだった | きれいではありません | きれいでは(じゃ)ない | きれいではありませんでした | きれいでは(じゃ)なかった.

6. When the -*na* adjective goes before the noun it describes, we keep な; but when it's placed before the verb です, we remove it.

解答

7. Nouns in Japanese have neither gender nor number. Yodo has offered Yasu a 宝石[ほうせき] ("jewel"), but she hasn't specified that it was only one. However, Yasu, upon hearing 宝石[ほうせき], thinks she will give him many, but when he sees it's only one he gets furious.

8. Counters are small auxiliary words used to tell "how many" things there are, and, thus, make up for the lack of a number indicator in nouns. 個[こ] is a counter used to "count" small and round things. More details in L.25.

9. くま, ライオン, 馬[うま], さる, 犬[いぬ], ぞう, 牛[うし], うさぎ.

10. 八百屋[やおや]: やさい｜本屋[ほんや]: ざっし｜肉屋[にくや]: にく｜文房具屋[ぶんぼうぐや]: かみ‖魚屋[さかなや]: 魚[さかな]｜果物屋[くだものや]: みかん｜電気屋[でんきや]: カメラ｜八百屋[やおや]: レタス｜レストラン: ごはん.

11. a) 黄色[きいろ]い｜b) いちご｜c) 白[しろ]い｜d) レモン｜e) 青[あお]い｜f) 赤[あか]い.

12. b) なしはやさいではありません｜c) りんごは赤[あか]い(黄色[きいろ]い)です｜d) ぞうは小[ちい]さくないです｜e) 日本の夏はさむくないです｜f) レモンは黄色[きいろ]いです.

13. 今[いま]、四時[よじ]です It's now four o'clock.｜今[いま]、十時半[じゅうじはん]です / 今[いま]、十時三十分[じゅうじさんじゅっぷん]です It's now half past ten.｜今[いま]、七時十五分[しちじじゅうごふん]すぎです / 今[いま]、七時十五分[しちじじゅうごふん]です It's now a quarter past seven.｜今[いま]、九時十五分[くじじゅうごふん]まえです / 今[いま]、八時四十五分[はちじよんじゅうごふん]です It's now a quarter to nine (eight forty-five).

14. b) 今[いま]、朝[あさ](午前[ごぜん])の七時半[しちじはん]です｜c) 今[いま]、深夜[しんや]の二時十五分[にじじゅうごふん]です｜d) 今[いま]、夕方[ゆうがた]の七時四十五分[しちじよんじゅうごふん](夕方[ゆうがた]の八時十五分[はちじじゅうごふん]まえ)です｜e) 今[いま]、朝[あさ](午前[ごぜん])の五時五十八分[ごじごじゅうはっぷん]です｜f) 今[いま]、夜[よる]の十時二十四分[じゅうじにじゅうよんぷん]です.

15. 1) This is a pig.｜2) This is a sow.｜3) These are pigs.｜4) These are sows.‖In Japanese, nouns have neither gender nor number, therefore, without a context, we cannot state whether there is one or several, or whether it is female or male.

16. a) 3. 小[ちい]さ｜b) 1. じゃ｜c) 3. 親切[しんせつ]｜d) 4. 暖[あたた]かい

17. b) 高[たか]くなかった｜c) きれいです｜d) 低[ひく]くないです｜e) 大[おお]きい｜f) 静[しず]かな / 好[す]きだ｜g) きらいではありませんでした.

18. b) この試験[しけん]はやさしくないです｜c) その馬[うま]は小[ちい]さかった｜d) あのたてものは安全[あんぜん]ではありませんでした｜e) 神戸[こうべ]の肉[にく]は安[やす]くなかったです｜f) 彼[かれ]は魚[さかな]がきらいだ｜g) 富士山[ふじさん]は低[ひく]くない山です｜h) 大阪[おおさか]のラーメン屋[や]は下手[へた]だ.

19. b) 川田[かわだ]さんは上手[じょうず]でした｜c) 川本[かわもと]さんはきれいな人[ひと]でした｜d) あのりんごは高[たか]かっ

たです｜e) その女はきれいではありません｜f) 山田さんの家は暗くない家です.

20. a) あの車は安くなかったです｜b) あれは有名なおかしやだ｜c) 私は暗い~~な~~教室がきらいではありません｜d) 山田さんの家は暗い家ではない (there are no mistakes)｜e) その安全じゃない~~な~~レストランは大きくなかった.

21. b) ちゃん｜c) 先生｜d) くん｜e) 殿｜f) 様｜g) 社長.

22. (Check the answer using the Compilation of Kanji in the textbook.)

23. 昼: ひる｜古い: ふるい｜青い: あおい｜朝: あさ｜夜: よる｜安い: やすい‖高い: たかい｜大きい: おおきい｜時: じ｜小さい: ちいさい｜赤い: あかい｜半: はん.

24. a) 2. 明るい｜b) 1. 今年｜c) 4. 白い｜d) 2. 新しい.

25. a) 2. ふるほん｜b) 4. すきな｜c) 3. ごぜん.

26. 五分: ごふん five minutes｜六分: ろっぷん six minutes｜三時半: さんじはん half past three｜高い: たかい high / expensive｜人前: ひとまえ in public｜前半: ぜんはん first part｜半分: はんぶん half｜青春: せいしゅん youth｜文明: ぶんめい civilization.

27. やすい: 安い cheap｜あさ: 朝 morning｜かた: 方 person (formal)｜おおきい: 大きい big｜いま: 今 now｜あかい: 赤い red｜ごご: 午後 afternoon｜せいねん: 青年 young person｜せきじゅう字: 赤十字 Red Cross.

28. 十万円 じゅうまんえん｜新しい あたらしい｜五時半 ごじはん｜高い たかい｜四分 よんぷん｜昼 ひる｜午後 ごご｜半分 はんぶん｜今月 こんげつ.

Block 4

1. Yodo uses the formal form when she speaks to Yasu; and Yasu uses the simple form when he speaks to Yodo. This reveals she respects him, partly because he is older, and probably because she also considers him a very powerful and fearful enemy. On the other hand, the use of the simple form by Yasu when he speaks to Yodo reveals he doesn't respect her much; in fact, he feels "superior" to her, and so he uses this form to intimidate her.

2. The first soldier is talking about another soldier (a person,) and that is why he uses いる (used with animate beings). The second soldier is talking about the object 弾 "(bullets)," and therefore he uses ある (used with objects and inanimate beings).

3. ヨド様！ヤス様はここにいる。ヤス様と話さないか？ The formal form is used because

the soldier's rank is lower than Yodo's, and he must show respect to his superior.

4. 話す, 話した, 話さない, 話さなかった, 話します, 話しました, 話しません, 話しませんでした
伝える, 伝えた, 伝えない, 伝えなかった, 伝えます, 伝えました, 伝えません, 伝えませんでした.

5. At the end of the sentence, the particle の is used to make informal questions. It's an informal version of か.

6. よ is used here as an emphatic marker, to give the sentence more expressive strength. ぞ has an identical function to that of よ, but it's much more vulgar, and only used by men in very informal situations.

7. Here, the grammatical function of the particle の is to indicate "possession" or "relationship." In this case, 休戦の条件, the "condition" (条件) belongs to a "truce" (休戦); in other words, "the condition(s) of the truce." を is used to mark the direct object, which receives the verb's action. Thus, in 休戦の条件を伝える, what is "conveyed" (伝える) are the "conditions of the truce" (休戦の条件).

8. へ is the particle for direction, it indicates "to where" something goes. Therefore, Yuki "goes" (出ます) "out" (外). と is used here to literally quote somebody else's words. In this case, the soldier literally quotes what Yuki has said: 外へ出ます "I (will) go outside."

9. Animals: からす | くじら | あり | はえ | しか | 馬 || Vegetables: じゃがいも | たまねぎ | ピーマン | かぼちゃ | レタス || Fruit: バナナ | もも | りんご | すいか | みかん || Stationary: ボールペン | ふで | 切手 | 紙 || Cutlery: フォーク | コップ | ナイフ | はし | 皿 || Stores: 本屋 | 八百屋 | パン屋 | くつ屋 | 肉屋 || Weather: 梅雨 | 秋 | 嵐 | 雪 | きり.

10. ベッド:起きる | 手紙:書く | ボール:遊ぶ | お茶:飲む | ケーキ屋:買う || 日本語:教える | ご飯:食べる | 本:書く | 人:呼ぶ | 家:帰る.

11. b) いる there is / are | c) いる to be | d) ある there is / are | e) ある to have | f) ある there is / are.

12. b) 行く | c) 食べる | d) 猫 | e) 飲む | f)スプーン / スープ | g) 読む | h) お金.

13. b) 犬はあそこにいなかった。| c) 私はざっしを読んだ。| d) 車で東京へ行った | e) あの山に川はありません。| f) さめは海にいない。| g) あなたはきれいな漢字を書いた。| h) 先生は私に日本語を教えます。

14. b) formal / both | c) colloquial / woman | d) colloquial / man | e) formal / both | f) vulgar / man.

15. a) 2．は / 1．の | b) 4．へ / 2．と | c) 3．で / 2．に / 1．を．

16. a) は / に | b) は / が | c) は / に / を | d) へ / で | e) に / と | f) の or に / を | g) に / を / に | h) で / と / と．

17. a) 私の名前はジョナサンです | b) 彼女は家にいる。しかし、教室で勉強する | c) フミコさんは電車でここへ来ますよ | d) 私はレストランでケーキを食べる．

18. ありました, ありません, ない, なかった | 食べます, 食べる, 食べませんでした, 食べなかった | 呼びました, 呼んだ, 呼びません, 呼ばない, 呼ばなかった | 持ちます, 持ちました, 持つ, 持ちませんでした, 持たなかった | 守ります, 守りました, 守った, 守りません, 守りませんでした, 守らない, 守らなかった．

19. b) 私の車は青いです | c) 先生は私と庭で遊んだ, or 私は先生と庭で遊んだ, or 私と先生は庭で遊んだ, or 先生と私は庭で遊んだ | d) あなたはりんごを食べましたか | e) 私は電車で家へ帰る | f) 彼の家はしずかですか．

20. a) あの鳥はケーキを食べなかった。 | b) 二時間前、彼女の家へ行きました。 | c) ここでやさいを買わない。 | d) 明日、社長とコーヒーを飲まない。

21. (Check the answer using the Compilation of Kanji in the textbook.)

22. 見る:みる | 右:みぎ | 売る:うる | 入る:はいる | 石:いし | 左:ひだり ‖ 外:そと | 思う:おもう | 買う:かう | 来る:くる | 出る:でる | 中:なか．

23. a) 2．帰る | b) 4．売春 | c) 3．持つ | d) 2．飲食．

24. a) 1．らいげつ / 2．きます | b) 3．かねもち / 4．はいった | c) 1．じかん / 3．みほん．

25. 出る:でる to go out | 右:みぎ right | 石:いし stone, rock | 教える:おしえる to teach | 行う:おこなう to hold, to carry out | 下がる:さがる to go down, to drop | 人間:にんげん person, human being | 朝食:ちょうしょく breakfast．

26. うえ:上 up | なか:中 center, inside | いく:行く to go | あいだ:間 between, interval | がいじん:外人 foreigner | おもう:思う to think | ちゅうねん:中年 middle age | やかん:夜間 during the night．

27. 持つ もつ or 待つ まつ | 下がる さがる or 上がる あがる | 飲む のむ | 左右 さゆう | 時間 じかん | 見る みる | 入る はいる | 売買 ばいばい | 昼食 ちゅうしょく．

解答

Block 5

1. Because Yasu had promised he would only dismantle the cannons outside the Saka base, and he actually had the inside ones dismantled as well, leaving the base defenseless. Insults: バカもの, ちくしょう, バカを言う, クソ親父 (おやじ) and くそ.

2. おじいさん literally means "grandfather," but is also used to refer to unknown old men, or, as in this chapter, simply to refer to elder men.

3. 10 outside and 6 inside. The counter 台 (だい), is used, because they are "machines." Trees are counted with 本 (because they are long and thin), and pigeons with 羽 (わ) (because they are considered animals which can fly or hop).

4. 弱く (よわく) (weakly), derived from 弱い (よわい) (weak); 静かに (しずかに) (quietly), derived from 静かな (しずかな) (quiet); and 深く (ふかく) (deeply), derived from 深い (ふかい) (deep).

5. ひどい: ひどく | 頑固な (がんこな): 頑固に (がんこに) | 遅い (おそい): 遅く (おそく)

6. もう: already | だけ: only | 少し (すこし): a little | とても: very.

7. やめて: simple form やめる, -masu form やめます, meaning "to stop," "to cease" (doing something) | して: する, します, "to do" | 考えて (かんがえて): 考える (かんがえる), 考えます (かんがえます), "to think" | 出して (だして): 出す (だす), 出します (だします), "to take out."

8. あやまっている | 従ってください (したがってください) | 負けていません (まけていません) | 壊していなかった (こわしていなかった).

9. 撤去する (てっきょする): -masu form 撤去します (てっきょします), -te form 撤去して (てっきょして), meaning "dismantle" | 約束する (やくそくする): 約束します (やくそくします), 約束して (やくそくして), "to promise."

10. He uses the word お母さん (おかあさん). It's more natural for a son to address his mother with お母さん (おかあさん). Using the words meant for somebody else's family to refer to members of your own family is quite common if the family member addressed is older than you.

11. 人: 兄 (あに), 先生 (せんせい), 男 (おとこ), 妻 (つま), 警察官 (けいさつかん), おじいさん, 母親 (ははおや) | 枚: 写真 (しゃしん), 紙 (かみ), 切手 (きって), ディスク, 手紙 (てがみ), 新聞 (しんぶん) | 台: 車 (くるま), パソコン, バス, カメラ, 自転車 (じてんしゃ), 電車 (でんしゃ), コンピュータ | 本: えんぴつ, ボールペン, ふで, 足 (あし), バナナ, 木 | 匹: 猫 (ねこ), あり, たこ, かえる, へび, さる | 頭: くま, ライオン, 馬 (うま), とら, ぞう, ぶた, 羊 (ひつじ) | 冊: 本, マンガ, 雑誌 (ざっし) | 個: すし, もも, ボール, オレンジ, いちご, ゴム, みかん.

12. b) 九個 (きゅうこ) (九つ (ここの)) | c) 八階 (はっかい) (八つ (やっ)), 何階 (なんがい) (いくつ) | d) 二人 (ふたり) (二つ (ふた)) | e) 四頭 (よんとう) (四つ (よっ)) | f) 六冊 (ろくさつ) (六つ (むっ)) | g) 三本 (さんぼん) (三つ (みっ)) | h) 一匹 (いっぴき) (一つ (ひと)).

13. おかあさん: はは | おっと: だんなさん | かない: おくさん | むすめさん: むすめ | あね:

おねえさん | そふ: おじいちゃん || パパ: とうちゃん | おふくろ: ははおや | おばさん: おば
あに: おにいさん | にょうぼう: つま | そほ: おばあさん.

14. b) 妹~~き方~~ | c) (correct) | d) ~~妻~~奥さん | e) (correct).

15. a) ４．昨日 | b) ２．上に | c) １．安く | d) ３．きっと | e) ４．上手に.

16. 見る, 見て, to look | 寝る, 寝て, to sleep | 急ぐ, 急いで, to hurry | 貸す, 貸して, to lend | 遊ぶ, 遊んで, to play | 呼ぶ, 呼んで, to call | 疲れる, 疲れて, to get tired | する, して, to do | 飲む, 飲んで, to drink | 教える, 教えて, to teach | 歌う, 歌って, to sing || 座る, 座って, to sit | 買う, 買って, to buy | 抱く, 抱いて, to hug | 行く, 行って, to go | 作る, 作って, to make | ある, あって, to be | 読む, 読んで, to read | 来る, 来て, to come | 走る, 走って, to run | 知る, 知って, to know | 死ぬ, 死んで, to die | 歩く, 歩いて, to walk.

17. b) 終わっていない | c) 笑ってください | d) 呼んでいる | e) 行ってください | f) 殺していません | g) 吸っています | h) 帰ってください | i) 飲んでいませんでした.

18. b) 前に | c) 早く | d) 昨日; 明日 | e) きっと; ちょっと | f) 小さく | g) 上手に.

19. b) 結婚していました | c) 勉強して(ください) | d) 運転しています | e) 出発していなかった.

20. a) の / に / と | b) へ (you can also use に) / で / で | c) は / で / と or の / を | d) と / が / と | e) に / の / が / に.

21. (Check the answer using the Compilation of Kanji in the textbook.)

22. 父: ちち | 妹: いもうと | 近い: ちかい | 遠い: とおい | 弟: おとうと | 多い: おおい || 体: からだ | 強い: つよい | 弱い: よわい | 家: いえ | 兄: あに | 姉: あね.

23. a) １．広い | b) ３．姉 | c) ４．会社 | d) １．父母.

24. a) ２．しょうねん / ４．なまえ | b) ４．とう / ３．しまい | c) １．おとうと / ３．げんき / １．か.

25. a) 会社: かいしゃ / 会いました: あいました | b) 天気: てんき / 家: いえ / 遠く: とおく | c) 社会: しゃかい / お兄さん: おにいさん | d) 体力: たいりょく / 体: からだ / 少し: すこし / 弱い: よわい / 休む: やすむ.

26. はは: 母 mother | ちから: 力 strength | ひろい: 広い wide | つよい: 強い strong | きゅうじつ: 休日 holiday | たぶん: 多分 perhaps | にんき: 人気 popular | きもち: 気持ち feeling.

27. 姉 あね | 気持ち きもち | 体力 たいりょく | 広大 こうだい | 人気 にんき | 会社 かいしゃ, o bien 社会 しゃかい | 少年 しょうねん | 力強い ちからづよい | 弟 おとうと.

Block 6

1. ただいま is the set phrase used by someone when entering his or her own house. Hide enters the Saka base (i.e., his own base); therefore, it's normal for him to use it. The soldier answers お帰りなさい, the greeting uttered by the person who is already inside to the person coming from outside.

2. If Hide went into Yasu's house he would say お邪魔します (in fact, that is exactly what Yuki does a few panels later). Yasu should answer いらっしゃい.

3. She has a headache (頭が痛いです). | "My back hurts:" 背中が痛いです | "I have an earache:" 耳が痛いです | "My knee hurts:" ひざが痛いです.

4. くたくた: to be exhausted *(gitaigo)* | いらいら: to be nervous, annoyed *(gitaigo)* | しっかり: to brace oneself up, to be stouthearted *(gitaigo)*.

5. 悲しくなる means to become sad, to be saddened | 便利になる: to become convenient | 深くなる: to deepen, to become deep | リーダーになる: to become a leader.

6. They add the nuance of "performing an action which does or receives a favor." | 話しに行ってあげてください: Please, go to speak to her (and, thus, do her a favor). | 行ってくれる？: Would you mind going (and, thus, doing me and/or someone close to me a favor)?

7. 呼ぶ: 呼べ, 呼びなさい | だまる: だまれ, だまりなさい | 許す: 許せ, 許しなさい | 待つ: 待て, 待ちなさい | 覚える: 覚えろ, 覚えなさい.

8. 呼びにいきます means "to go to call (somebody)." | だまりにいく | 許しにいく | 待ちにいく | 覚えにいく.

9. 頭がいい: "to be intelligent." | 腕がいい: "to be very good at something."

10. Head: ひたい, 歯, 耳, 鼻, 目, ほお, 頭, 口, まつげ, かみの毛, 舌, ひげ, あご, 顔 | Torso: 肩, 背中, 胸, おなか, へそ | Limbs: うで, ひじ, 足, ひざ, 足元 | Hand: 親指, 指, 爪, 人差し指, 中指, 手の平, 小指. | **Note:** 手首 and 手 can both go under "hand" and "limbs." Any of the two options is correct. Likewise, のど and 首 can both go under "head" and "torso."

11. 1: e | 2: i | 3: b | 4: g | 5: k | 6: j | 7: a | 8: d | 9: c | 10: h | 11: f

12. a) 2. げらげら | b) 4. どきどき | c) 1. すっきり | d) 1. ぺこぺこ | 3. ぱくぱく.

13. a: よろしくお願いします | b: かみの毛 | c: しくしく | d: おじ | e: 馬 | f: だんな | g: 目 | h: おばあさん | i: おかえりなさい | j: さる | k: お腹 | l: 祖母 | m: 薬指 | n: ぺらぺら.

14. 行け, 行きなさい, 行ってくれ, 行くな, "to go" | 回れ, 回りなさい, 回ってくれ, 回るな, "to go around" | 読め, 読みなさい, 読んでくれ, 読むな, "to read" | 貸せ, 貸しなさい, 貸してくれ, 貸すな, "to lend" | 触れ, 触りなさい, 触ってくれ, 触るな, "to touch" | 洗え, 洗いなさい, 洗ってくれ, 洗うな, "to wash" | 教えろ, 教えなさい, 教えてくれ, 教えるな, "to teach" | 呼べ, 呼びなさい, 呼んでくれ, 呼ぶな, "to call" | 狙え, 狙いなさい, 狙ってくれ, 狙うな, "to aim (at)" | 死ね, 死になさい, 死んでくれ, 死ぬな, "to die" | 走れ, 走りなさい, 走ってくれ, 走るな, "to run" | 急げ, 急ぎなさい, 急いでくれ, 急ぐな, "to hurry."

15. b) gives: アケミ, receives: 私 | c) gives: 弟, receives: お母さん | d) gives: テツ, receives: クミ | e) da: 山本, receives: モモコ | f) gives: 学生, receives: 私 | g) gives: 山田, receives: 兄.

16. b) 遊び | c) 好きに | d) よく | e) 読んで

17. a) 3. 洗え | b) 1. 買い | c) 4. で | d) 3. くれました | e) 3. 来なさい | f) 3. 早く | g) 1. 来い | h) 2. が | i) 4. 見るな.

18. (Check the answer using the Compilation of Kanji in the textbook.)

19. 国: くに | 口: くち | 心: こころ | 足: あし | 車: くるま | 耳: みみ || 目: め | 変: へん | 生: なま | 道: みち | 手: て | 店: みせ.

20. a) 1. 楽しい | b) 2. 学生 | c) 3. 学校 | d) 3. 外国.

21. a) 3. だいがく / 4. ともだち / 3. せんせい | b) 4. ちゅうごくご / 2. あんしん | c) 1. こうこうせい / 2. いきている.

22. a) 先月: せんげつ / 遠足: えんそく / 楽しかった: たのしかった | b) 出口: でぐち / 売店: ばいてん / 先: さき / 道: みち / 車: くるま | c) 私立学校: しりつがっこう / 中学生: ちゅうがくせい / 自白: じはく | d) 赤道: せきどう / 楽: らく / 近道: ちかみち / 言って: いって.

23. くち: 口 mouth | みみ: 耳 ear | あし: 足 foot, leg | じんせい: 人生 life | たのしい: 楽しい pleasant | にほんご: 日本語 Japanese language | ぼこく: 母国 native country | ぶんめい: 文明 civilization.

24. 変わる かわる | 先月 せんげつ | 手足 てあし | 学ぶ まなぶ | 立つ たつ | 大変 たいへん | 中心 ちゅうしん | 自分 じぶん | 入口 いりぐち.

For 1st and 2nd edition holders

In 2006 the expanded and corrected edition of *Japanese in MangaLand* was published. The new edition meant a radical improvement in the design of the inside pages, while the contents themselves hardly varied. However, some explanations are more complete, and, occasionally, there are a few additional explanations.

So that the owners of the old edition can use this exercise book without any problem, we offer this extra material.

Block 1

⇒ 1 億: 100.000.000 (one hundred million).

Block 2

⇒ せっしゃ: "I," used by samurais in olden times. | われわれ: "we," formal. | 俺ら: "we," vulgar.

⇒ Transcription of the "x" sound: クス. Example: ファックス (*fax*).

⇒ Demonstrative *kosoado*: この (this), その (that), あの (that over there), どの (which?). Example: この犬は大きいです, "This dog is big."

Block 3

⇒ Additional vocabulary: 犬: dog | 猫: cat | 鳥: bird | 馬: horse | 牛: cow / bull | さる: monkey | うさぎ: rabbit | 羊: sheep | へび: snake | ぶた: pig | 魚: fish | くま: bear | あり: ant | ライオン: lion | ぞう: elephant | しか: deer | とら: tiger | りゅう: dragon | からす: crow | くじら: whale | バナナ: banana | りんご: apple | なし: pear | すいか: watermelon | オレンジ: orange | みかん: mandarin | いちご: strawberry | レモン: lemon | もも: peach | トマト: tomato | じゃがいも: potato | たまねぎ: onion | レタス: lettuce | ピーマン: pepper | きのこ: mushroom | にんにく: garlic | かぼちゃ: pumpkin | まめ: bean | 皿: dish | フォーク: fork | スプーン: spoon | ナイフ: knife.

⇒ Time adverbs: 午前 or 朝: morning | 昼: noon | 午後: afternoon | 夕方: evening | 夜: night | 深夜: midnight.

⇒ Besides suffixes for proper names, using "titles" after a name is also very common. Examples: 先生: professor, doctor | 夫人: Mrs. | 社長: company director | 課長: section head | 部長: head of department | 選手: player, athlete.

Block 4

There is nothing to mention in this block.

Block 5

⇒ In colloquial Japanese, one tends to use the words meant for somebody else's family to refer to those members of one's own family who are older than the speaker. Calling your father お父さん or your mother お母さん instead of 母 or 父 (the formal options) is very normal.

⇒ Synonyms. "One's own husband:" だんな, 主人〔しゅじん〕, 夫〔おっと〕 | "One's own wife:" 家内〔かない〕, 女房〔にょうぼう〕, 妻〔つま〕.

Block 6

⇒ Set phrases. 腕〔うで〕がいい: To be very good at something | 頭〔あたま〕がいい: To be intelligent.

⇒ Translating くれる as "to give (me)," is better, even though it has a component implying "to receive." It's used when somebody "gives" something "to me" or "to somebody (psychologically) close to me" (it can be either a relative, somebody in my class, office, group, etc.). The *kureru* part in the table, then, would be better this way:

くれる *kureru* "to give"	Xは私にZをくれる *x wa watashi ni z o kureru* Mr. x gives z to me (x: gives / I: receive)	鈴木君は私にワインをくれる *Suzuki-kun wa watashi ni wain o kureru* Suzuki (suf.) TOP I IOP wine DOP give Suzuki gives me wine.

⇒ The negative imperative is obtained by just adding な after a verb in the dictionary form. For example: 食〔た〕べる "to eat:" 食〔た〕べるな "don't eat."

⇒ The 〜てくれ form is an imperative variation of the 〜てくれる (L.28, somebody does me or somebody close to me a favor). The 〜てくれ form (combination of a verb conjugated in the *-te* form plus くれ, the imperative of くれる) is a quite rough imperative, and is used to give direct orders. For example: この本〔ほん〕を読〔よ〕んでくれ, "Read this book (come on!)" or "Do me the favor of reading this book."

注意!
WATCH OUT!!

YOU HAVE JUST OPENED THIS BOOK
THE OTHER WAY AROUND!!!

This workbook is written in the true style of Japanese manga.
So, you must start reading from what would be the
last page; in the opposite direction, from right to left!